Manchester Thieftakers

Manchester Thieftakers

Don Hale

Manchester Thieftakers
First published in Wales
by
Bridge Books
61 Park Avenue
Wrexham
LL12 7AW

© 2007 Text Don Hale
© 2007 Typesetting and design Bridge Books

A CIP data entry for this book is available from the British Library

ISBN 978-1-84494-041-7

For a full list of Bridge Books publications visit our website

www.bridgebooks.co.uk

Printed and bound by
Cromwell Press Ltd
Trowbridge

Contents

Introduction

I always remember being in awe of my great-grandfather, James Wood, for decades without really quite understanding why. Any mention of his name at the dinner-table soon attracted coughs, grunts and weird stares, followed by a vigorous shaking of heads. It was the 'children must be seen but not heard' syndrome. For the best part of half a century, a rather dominant, yet dark, dour and dismal portrait of him, dressed in his rippled-effect, military style uniform, hung on the landing of my grandparents' home at Cleveleys, near Blackpool. It always reminded me of Lord Kitchener's haunting face from the famous Great War recruitment posters, with a large handlebar type moustache, and those jet-black penetrating eyes that seemed to follow you around, and made you keep turning back to see if he was still watching. As a child, it seemed quite scary and probably left a rather fearsome impression on my vulnerable young mind. I always presumed it was a reminder of his wartime service; but, nearly twenty years later discovered the picture actually commemorated his appointment as the youngest Superintendent at that time for Manchester City Police. Regrettably, this large picture has since disappeared, although some smaller copies remain, together with other softer and more flattering photographs of the man.

It seemed odd in later years, when I realised that Letitia, James's widow, and my great-grandmother, still protected his possessions with a fierce and passionate determination, converting her private room into a near shrine to his memory more than fifty years after James's death.

I recall the room as always being very dark, heavily scented and draped in long flowing black fabrics. It was also packed with memorabilia from their life together, and from his extraordinary career. Letitia always seemed exactly as she was, someone slightly out of place, from another time, another world! She was a very trim and petite

Facing: Superintendent James Wood.

lady, desperate to cling to her treasured memories. At home, she seemed to be in constant mourning and wore long dark clothes and a shawl or bonnet, and was wafer-thin with soft, delicate, wrinkled skin. The memory plays tricks as one gets older but Letitia seemed to me to move around as if she was on casters, and I can never recall her showing any great emotion. She kept herself to herself and was always a very proud and very private person, who had been widowed for such an intolerable time. She only appeared in public on very rare occasions, as if by prior appointment, and enjoyed most of her meals alone.

I was always inquisitive and perhaps fortunate to gain the very occasional brief chat with her amidst the many competing and ticking clocks, dusty ornaments and clinking glassware. Despite her rather abrupt manner, I could not help but like her. She had a very dry sense of humour, and enjoyed twice-weekly sessions of ballroom dancing at a small friendship club somewhere down past the tram tracks; continuing her hobby until the last few years of her life — claiming she only stopped due to a lack of suitable company, rather than any lack of mobility.

I eventually came across the old family photographs within some dusty, half-hidden boxes and 'secret' files of family archive material passed down the generations following the loss of my parents. When I examined the contents it seemed like stepping back in time, and raised so many questions that unfortunately no surviving family member could ever answer. I kept wondering why so many key issues had never been discussed before and felt disappointed that much of his material had remained a secret for so long. The information, however, certainly provided me with the inspiration to review many myths and rumours, and investigate a number of claims, in order to finally establish the truth about his remarkable life and career. Additional research, and the discovery of other archive records, allowed me to finally piece together a rather fascinating jigsaw, not just about my great grandfather, but also about major changes to social life around Manchester prior to 1914.

Quite incredibly, some other family papers related to James's own great-grandfather, James Wood (senior), had also survived in the form of a Watchman's Record Book for the period 1825–33. It provides a detailed, accurate and compelling account of street life in and around Longsight, Gorton, Ardwick and Ancoats several years before Robert

Peel's new 'Bobbies' came into being. The Watchmen however, remained the eyes and ears of the city for at least another ten years after Peel's introductions, and it was certainly at least eight years after the last entry in this record book before the police began to patrol the same Manchester patch and suburban streets.

The book not only tells of the daily grind of survival, of constant Watch patrols and criminal incidents, but it also adds some colour and flavour to what life was really like in Manchester at that time – and especially after dark! The incidents covered a varied and wide range of matters and were based on reports from about sixteen watchmen and several supervisors, including many from James Wood (senior) who was involved as a senior watch supervisor. Many of the documents were of little or no monetary value, but their historical importance is priceless and surprisingly, most have been extremely well preserved. All the entries were neat and hand-written, mainly in black ink with the dates and remarks clearly displayed. The actual book has now been donated to Manchester Police Museum.

James Wood (junior) spent fourteen years with Queen Victoria's Army, and a further twenty-four years with Manchester City Police. During his career in the force, he worked in all departments, and at one time was a detective sergeant working with Jerome Caminada, who was one of the city's most famous Victorian detectives. James became a highly proficient policeman, earning many plaudits for arrests and convictions and was a proud instigator and enforcer of changes in legislation relating to street trading laws, the licensing of theatrical children and the registration of servants. He also helped organise, supervise or became involved with a host of major city events, including the *Daily Mail* Air Race and the arrival of the very first 'flying machine.' He was also involved with Manchester United's name change – and their later move to Old Trafford – and with several memorable Royal visits including that of the Prince and Princess of Wales when he acted as the Royal bodyguard. In addition, he retained a close association with many of the personalities of the day, including Lord Northcliffe, Prime Minister Arthur Balfour and railway engineer Sir Nigel Gresley.

James was also responsible for the protection of many other prominent visiting VIPs, and for nearly a decade was the city's explosives officer at a time of great international drama and political unrest, with threats against the monarchy and government from 'Foreign Agents and Agitators,' and the British Army constantly engaged in overseas conflicts.

This book takes the raw seeds of discovery and converts them into a rich harvest of nostalgia and memorabilia. It also provides a unique insight and a remarkable 'behind the scenes' look at some of Manchester's major historical moments during a period of rapid development.

Unfortunately, James died at an early age, and yet, the impact of his work was such at that time, with so many wanting to pay a final tribute, that his slow funeral cortège practically brought the city to a standstill. This book is primarily written to commemorate the 140th anniversary of his birth. I believe it is now time to review the contents of his secret files and appreciate the sacrifice that he, and many other others, made to help establish Manchester's proud heritage.

Don Hale, OBE
2007

Acknowledgements

I would like to express my sincere thanks to my wife, Kath, and several members of my close family, for enduring many missing hours spent researching, travelling or busy writing up my notes for this book.

A special note of thanks too to my elder brother, Geoffrey, and his family, for help with preserving some valuable archive material; and belated thanks to my late parents, and grandparents, for ensuring that many irreplaceable and interesting items survived the decades for subsequent examination.

My grateful thanks to the Manchester City Council Library & Information Services Department, the Manchester City Archives Department and the Greater Manchester Police Museum for allowing the use of many previously unpublished, important and nostalgic photographs and illustrations.

In addition, I would like to thank the following people and organisations for their help with my research, and apologies to anyone else that may have helped in any way, but may have been omitted from this list in error. Every contribution, no matter how large or small, is fully appreciated.

- Duncan Broady, curator of the Greater Manchester Police Museum and Newton Street, and all his colleagues.
- Ms Paula Moorhouse, Manchester Archivist.
- The editor, *The Manchester Guardian & Manchester Evening News*.
- The editor, *The Times*, London.
- The editor, *Blackley Guardian*.
- The editor, *Oldham Evening Chronicle*.
- The London & North Western Railway Society.
- Ms Debbie Freeman, author of the Victorian play *Fire in the Park*.

- The Wise Monkey Theatre Company.
- The Police History Society.
- The New Moston History Society.
- The Manchester United Supporters Club and the Red Café.

All photographs, unless otherwise credited, are from the Wood family archives.

1. Early Watchmen & Special Constables

The very first written reference to 'law and order' relates to a Justices of the Peace title which was highlighted in the famous Magna Carta of 1215. An early listing of the word 'constable' appears in archive documents, with a reference to *Comes Stabuli* recorded in 1252, believed to relate to a 'master of a horse,' and meant someone of authority and control within the community. In 1285, a new Law of Enforcement was formulated and adopted as part of the Statute of Winchester. This was seen as the first legislation relating to a form of policing formally introduced and defined the office of a constable who was to answer directly to the Justice of the Peace. The justices, who were deemed the ruling authority of each county, were early forms of magistrates, and could issue warrants which were executed by constables. The justices generally appointed up to four officers to help them keep order.

During the sixteenth century all males aged between sixteen and sixty, were expected to assist with keeping the King's Peace and could be held jointly responsible for any outbreak of crime, violence, riot or public order offences. Then, it was also the duty of all citizens to keep arms (which generally meant carrying a sword, staff, dagger, or other weapon), with men being forced to attend any 'hue and cry' to trace criminals. Any man who failed to attend this call, could expect to find himself in the dock, and standing trial.

In 1673, King Charles II decreed that 'Special Constables' should be sworn-in and given unique responsibilities for maintaining law and order. The rank was a compulsory duty, rather than a voluntary act, and was certainly not to be taken lightly, or ignored. Anyone summoned to appear before a magistrate to be sworn in had to accept all the terms and conditions of service. A refusal, for whatever reason, could lead to a heavy fine, imprisonment or both! It was at this time that 'Night Watchmen' were introduced who could support the constables and patrol the streets of London after dark, to ensure law and order was maintained. It was the duty of the constable to set the night watch and the practice was later copied by many other major cities.

Policing in many other parts of the country, and particularly in the more rural areas, was organised by the Parish Constable or Parish Watchman. Initially, their ranks were filled by retired soldiers, and later by slightly disabled, wounded, elderly or needy men of the parish. In many cases, some of the watchmen were forced to attend to their duties, being considered 'charity cases' of the Parish. The agreement was that they undertook this type of work in exchange for food and shelter.

Some early London Watchmen resembled coachmen in appearance and wore three-cornered hats, long heavy grey-coats and capes. They also carried a pikestaff and an oil-filled lantern so that they could see their way around the dark cobbled streets, and carried a wooden staff for self-protection. In addition, they carried rattles (known as rick-racks) and a truncheon. The rattle was an instrument specifically designed to attract attention and summon assistance. In the main, they were fairly small and could be tucked into a watchman's belt. They consisted of a short wooden handle, joined with a body formed by a taught spring and two revolving cogs that clattered against each other when held above the head and swung around. It made a very noisy, rattling, 'rick-rack' sound. In certain trouble spots, the worried watchman would often walk along tapping his staff hard on the cobbles to warn of his approach, hoping he would not be attacked.

Night watchmen were designated specific areas to patrol and many even had their own small watch boxes in which to shelter from the winter weather. They resembled the 'Dr Who-type' police boxes of today. At times these boxes became the target for attacks from vandals and aggrieved villains, with several being destroyed by fire once the watchman left to attend to his rounds. Most watch boxes and rounds were situated in fairly close proximity to each other, and in case of need, the watchmen could 'rick' for assistance to alert their neighbours and colleagues. This noise, however, also tended to draw an enthusiastic crowd, anxious to see what was happening. The action sometimes resulted in other spectators joining in which often made matters worse.

In the early eighteenth century, a parish constable's role improved and appointments were made on a temporary basis, sometimes just for twelve months. Holders were required to be of smart appearance and have a reasonable grasp of the law of the land, and the position could be given to men of wealth and influence. They were generally unpaid and involved long hours of duty and responsibility. Some wealthy individuals paid to avoid this burden, as a year away from their business dealings could be devastating to their finances; if a constable was not able to attend to his duties, for whatever reason, it was his responsibility to appoint a deputy, although certain substitutes often proved highly unreliable.

The role of the constable was noted in church records as being one of four important local officers (the others being the surveyor of the highways, the churchwarden and the overseer of the poor) appointed annually to deal with parish matters. The precise position and title of the parish constable varied across the country, and at times nearly disappeared altogether from the ranks of importance, particularly during the latter part of that century. This impacted more within some of the larger cities, where other more prominent measures had to be taken to deal with the effects of the Industrial Revolution on communities. In more rural areas, however, the changes were less noticeable, and a constable continued to remain an essential member of the parish for decades.

On occasions, the constable had to detain a prisoner in his or her own home, until a magistrate was available to hear the charge. When the official arrived, many cases were eventually heard in the local inn. Sentences naturally varied, dependent upon the crime, and convicted persons faced immediate retribution. The courts were also a great source of public entertainment and offenders could be quickly taken out into the street and flogged, birched, fined or placed in the local stocks for public humiliation. The more serious offences of murder led to hanging from the gallows at the town gaols, which again were open to public spectacle and generally drew large crowds.

These early constables had no uniform, yet wore an armband and carried a wooden truncheon, with one or the other bearing a coat of arms, or colours of the parish. The officers were not always the most popular men in the district and often faced both serious attack and abuse. They were also open to bribery and corruption, with some reputed to turn an occasional blind eye to misdemeanours. Victims too, often had a very hard time in persuading both the constable and magistrate that an offence had been committed.

Many victims had to rely on professional 'thief-takers', hired heavy-duty assistants, many with ex-military backgrounds, who worked for cash rewards and were the equivalent of today's bounty hunters. In many cases, this was sometimes the only way to apprehend a known villain or violent criminal.

Thief-Takers too, faced similar temptations from corruption, with a greater prize sometimes offered to let the accused go. And these hunters also faced attacks from organised gangs, desperate to maintain the freedom of one of their members or another celebrated individual. Extreme poverty and rapid changes to work requirements and housing caused by the industrial revolution, increased pressures on the watchmen and parish constables, and soon the authorities demanded a more reliable and professional service.

The night watchman's work was poorly paid and usually meant patrolling slum dwellings and other poverty-stricken areas. Their services were also demanded on market days, carnivals or at local festivals, when the threat of trouble by visiting rogues and pick pockets increased. The hours of service were from 9 p.m. until 6 a.m., when they were required to patrol the streets throughout the hours of darkness. They were expected to walk their rounds at two and half miles per hour, and were not allowed to sit down on duty or lean upon anything, and were told to make minimal use of their watch boxes. If a town was under threat from organised gangs, the parish constable could summon additional special constables, as volunteers; and once again, refusal to attend to a constable's request was an offence punishable by imprisonment.

In many major cities during the early to mid 1800s there was tremendous fear, uncertainty and intense anger on the streets after dark, and wealthy businessmen again opted to hire their own watchmen to help protect both property and person. Many of these men again came from military backgrounds and carried an assortment of weapons. Some even resembled pirates with a large cutlass and a bull's-eye type lantern. They had specific duties and were only responsible to their own paymaster – as distinct from the parish constable or night watchman, whose duty was to keep the King's Peace.

Life in many industrial towns was extremely harsh with poverty and disease rife. Slums provided the greatest source of crime and if mobs rioted, the authorities were able to call on the militia for support. The militia also provided a welcome bonus to the cash-strapped responsibilities of the city governors, because if soldiers attended, they would be utilised at no cost to the local authority. A magistrate, or government official, had to authorise the use of the militia and at times read the Riot Act at public demonstrations, prior to instructing sabre-carrying guardsmen, who were called upon to quickly quell public violence and re-establish law and order.

The Old Watchman's Record Book, 1825–33
For many, the life of a watchman must have been a stark and lonely existence, particularly in winter, patrolling a tough beat in some desolate slum areas. The record book reveals something of the constant dangers of the job and makes occasional comment about missing watchmen, drunk and disorderly officers, and others who were constantly absent without leave. The areas covered included: New Gorton Road; Hyde Road; Ashton Road; Ashton Lane; Stockport Road; Chancery Lane; The Green; Chapel Street; Ardwick Road; Union Street; Chorlton Row; Pin Mill Brow; and many, many others.

The watchmen mentioned in the book were obviously based around the Gorton, Longsight, Ardwick and Ancoats areas, and the reports highlight many local pubs, hostelries and unauthorised drinking establishments, probably long demolished. Some include: the George & Dragon, the Blacksmith's Arms, the General Brick, Ancoats Hall and the Polygon. There are also details of Wakes activities in the Longsight, Ardwick and Stockport areas.

The record book provides the actual names and addresses of the watchmen employed throughout that period, with comments and remarks about their performances. The reports are written by several watchmen and their supervisors, and often tell us something of the occupations and activities of the inhabitants of the suburbs and cover incidents at the lime kiln works, the brick works, the paper mill, the bake house, the slaughter house, as well as various farms and orchards. It seems a remarkable contrast within the space of a few miles from heavy industrial sites to rural settings.

The record also mentions the work of the lamp lighter, and the damage caused by strong winds and storms. It was part of the night watchmen's duties to ensure that lamps were lit and to report any damage on the darkened streets. They were also instructed to check for unfastened window shutters, doors and gates, with instructions to wake the occupants if any were found to be un-tethered. This was a particular concern in the summer months and no doubt caused aggravation between the house owners, servants and watchmen.

The entries in the book tell their own story and cover a wide range of unlawful activities, monitored by the officers, who always seemed to come in for extreme criticism – and yet were expected to help keep the peace and satisfy the demands of local businessmen. Many entries cover people being drunk and disorderly as well as theft, forgery, highway robbery, horse stealing, sheep stealing, general rustling (and a theft of ducks), apple stripping and vagrancy. Some of these occurred on a regular basis and the officers certainly needed their wits about them to be able to make arrests. There are also reports of 'ricks' (the use of wooden police rattles) for assistance and mentions of injury and fires, which all had to be dealt with by the watchmen.

There were also many reports of the theft of clothing and food in the more poverty-stricken areas, together with shouts of murder, wife-beating, aggravated assaults, ferret hunting, threats to shoot, attacks with bricks and stones, poaching and the stealing of whisky.

Record book dates include:

18 July 1825 – 30 September 1825 — entries completed by James Wood, Senior.

9 October 1825 – 24 April 1828 — entries completed by Thomas Chantler.

30 April 1830 – 18 May 1830 — entries mainly completed by Richard Nicholson, with many others unsigned.

2 August 1831 – 30 July 1833 — many are unsigned but one, dated 12 September 1831, was signed by Alsibrook Sampson.

Names and residence of watchmen:

N° 1. Henry Vaudrey, Coach Alley.

N° 2. George Grimshaw, 13 Berry Street.

N° 3. James Smith, William Street.

N° 4. Joshua Barnes, 56 Loom Street, Newton Lane.

N° 5. John Royle, Back William Street.

N° 6. Thomas Gardner, Back Chapel, Chancery Lane.

Additional and updated changes:
   Nº 4. Samuel Woolley, Chapel Street.
   Nº 5. John Parry, No 3 Chandler Street.
   Nº 4. James Foster, Robinson Court, Back Chapel Street.
   Nº 6. John Andrew, Back Chapel Street.
   Nº 3. John Dollaghan, Bench Street.

Other watchmen listed within the reports were: William Broom; George Kay; William Heywood; Robert Carter; William Jones; John Ryley; and Thomas Pimblott.

Although the reports contain few references to major crimes (although murder and assault do appear), they are of great interest in that they show the wide range of incidents that were dealt with by the watchmen including: burglary, sheep stealing, stray animals, drunken disorderliness, fighting as well as the nightly security checks on premises. Also of interest are the references to drunkeness amongst the watchmen themselves.

Monday evening, July 18th 1825.
   Dist 4. Joshua Barnes absent.
Tuesday morning, July 19th 1825.
   I visited the watchmen during the night and found them alert on their rounds. No reports.
   Tuesday evening, July 19th 1825.
   Dist 4. Joshua Barnes absent.
Wednesday morning, July 20th 1825.
   Dist 2. James Smith says that at two o'clock a woman cried out 'murder' near the Watch Box. He immediately pursued a man who made his escape. He returned back to the place and the woman was gone also. I visited the watchmen during the night and found them alert and on their rounds.
   Thursday morning, July 21st & Friday morning July 22nd 1825.
   I visited the watchmen during the night and found them alert and on their rounds. No reports.
Saturday morning, July 23rd 1825.
   Dist 5. John Royle says that he found the doors of Mr Shand, King's Head, Chancery Lane, open at three o'clock this morning and all gone to bed.
Sunday morning, July 24th 1825.

I visited the watchmen during the night and found them alert and on the rounds. A great number of drunk and disorderly people returning from the New Gorton Road between the hours of one and two o'clock in the morning.

Dist 6. William Broom says that ongoing his ten o'clock round last night the landlord of the George & Dragon public house insulted him wherein the execution of his duty.

Wednesday morning, July 27th 1825.

Dist 5. John Royle reports that at six o'clock last night, he saw two boys, Jack Bates and Charlie Hyde, lobbing the garden of Mr Turner. He took them into custody and brought them to the lock-up. The comments in the report book confirmed: They were publicly whipped on the Green and discharged on July 28th.

Sunday morning, July 31st 1825.

Dist 6. William Broom reports that between nine & ten o'clock last night, six men on the Ashton Road attempted to stop two gentlemen on horseback. The first put spurs to his horse and rode to Mr Jakes sign of General Brick; also, that a horse was found with a saddle and bridle - which was afterwards owned by a Mr Ashton of Blackburn. He stated that he was thrown off at the time of mounting. Broom further stated that he found a strayed cow about half past twelve o'clock on the same road - claimed by Mr Renshaw the following morning.

He also reports that at two o'clock, four men on Ancoats Bridge were breaking the peace and told to go home, but did not. He 'ricked' and they dispersed. Also reports by Joshua Norris, Flag Alley, keeping a disorderly house and at the same time, his wife abusing him and watchman Ryley.

Dist 2. James Smith reports that at half past one o'clock, a very disorderly gang of people was assembled on the Green from Chapel Street. That he and Kay went to disperse them and they gave battle – Chorlton Watchmen came to their assistance and one watchman was very much abused. Two were known, James Wright and Elias Gregson with Dan Howard of Chapel Street.

Remarks: Warrant obtained for James Wright and apprehended on Monday and called to answer at Sessions on Tuesday 2nd inst. Elias Gregson left town.

I visited the watchmen during the night and found George Kay intoxicated – a great deal of disorderly people at two o'clock and three men on the Stockport Road with six ducks in a shirt. On seeing me the men ran back towards Longsight and I sprung my rattle and they dropped the ducks.

In his remarks, it confirmed: Six ducks were owned by a Mr Deane of Chorlton Road and delivered to his man on Monday morning.

Monday morning, August 1st 1825.

Dist 6. William Broom in liquor when going on.

Tuesday morning, August 2nd 1825.

A great deal of disorderly people through the night returning from Longsight Wakes. At ten o'clock, Mr Hardy brought the prisoners to the lock-ups; one for fighting, and the other for rescuing another. James Murray for fighting, William Mark for rescue.

Dist 2. James Smith reports that at half past ten o'clock, he found a very disorderly set of people in Chapel Street, he took Thomas Howarth into custody.

Remarks: James Murray and William Mark committed for warrant of bail on August 2nd. Thomas Howarth discharged on August 2nd.

Wednesday morning, August 3rd 1825.

At a quarter to ten o'clock, John Bromley of Hooley Hill, Ashton, was bathing in Ardwick Pond. I was under the necessity of sending his clothes to the office before he could be persuaded to come out. George Kay reports he had been in for some time.

When I came up, a great number of disorderly people coming from Longsight watched. Robert Simmons brought to the lock-up by Thomas Hulme for fighting.

Remarks: Bromley discharged on 3rd August. Simmons committed for warrant of bail on August 3rd. He was sent before the Commissioners on same day.

Saturday morning, August 6th 1825.

Dist 2. James Smith reports that two men were fighting on his round at twelve o'clock. He took James Nettleton into custody and brought him to the lock-up.

Dist 6. William Broom reports that he found two strayed lambs at three o'clock and left them at Mr Barker's farm opposite the George & Dragon on Ashton Road. They were later claimed by Mr Brogden from near Ancoats Hall on August 7th.

Remarks: Nettleton was discharged on August 6th.

Sunday morning, August 7th 1825.

At twelve o'clock John Royle and William Broom were arguing with a Mr Maskery.

Wednesday morning, August 10th, 1825.

Dist 4. Joshua Barnes reports that at half past ten o'clock he was called into a house at the Crescent to turn a drunken woman out.

Dist 5. John Royle reports that at half past twelve o'clock were in Mr Buchan's garden. On his approaching, they ran through the brick crofts towards Gorton Road.

Sunday morning, August 14th 1825.

Dist 2. James Smith reports that at one o'clock, he found a respectable looking man very drunk near to the box, who stated that he had been robbed of five sovereigns – and later said two sovereigns – by two men. One stopped his mouth. He said he was going to Stockport.

Dist 5. John Royle reports that William Owen, Chancery Lane, has three Saturday nights come home drunk, broke the peace and behaved himself very disorderly at a late hour, and when desired to be quieter, used very improper language to him.

Monday, Tuesday and Wednesday mornings, August 15th, 16th & 17th 1825.

I visited the watchmen during the night and found them alert on their rounds. No reports. Remarks: On Wednesday, August 17th, I went to Lancaster to give evidence on a case of forgery on the Mirfield Bank near Huddersfield. Returned Monday, 22nd inst.

Tuesday morning, August 23rd 1825.

1st round from ten till half past eleven. All alert. 2nd round from twelve to a quarter to two. All alert. 3rd round from three to a quarter past four. All alert. George Kay reports that a little before ten o'clock, a man named Tinker who lives in Chapel Street, was very disorderly on the Green.

Wednesday morning, August 24th 1825.

I visited the watchmen at the under mentioned times:

1st round from half past ten till one o'clock. John Royle reports that at twelve o'clock a gang of young men were singing and making a great noise in Chancery Lane. He desired them to be quiet and go away. They then began to threaten and beat him.

2nd round from half past one to half past two o'clock. All alert. 3rd round from three to a quarter part four. All alert. Remarks: Heard before the Commission on Wednesday evening, the 24th inst.

Thursday morning, August 25th 1825.

I visited the watchmen during the night at the under mentioned times:

1st round from ten till twelve o'clock. All alert. 2nd round from twelve till two o'clock. All alert. 3rd round from three till half past four o'clock. All alert.

Friday morning, August 26th 1825.

1st round from half past ten to half past twelve o'clock. William Broom neglected to go the upper part of his rounds on the Ashton Road at eleven o'clock; 2nd round, from half past twelve to half past two o'clock. William Broom neglected to go on the upper part of his round on the Ashton Road at ten o'clock and also at two o'clock; 3rd round from half past two to a quarter to five o'clock. No reports on this round.

Saturday morning, August 27th 1825.

Mr Dean of Chorlton Row says that two men had been larking about his premises and that a tree was stripped of apples. Joshua Barnes chased them across the fields.

Sunday, Monday and Tuesday mornings, August 28th, 29th & 30th August 1825.

Round times varied. Monday: James Smith reports that a back door of one of the new buildings in Tipping Street had been broken open during Sunday. No other reports.

From Wednesday morning, August 31st, until Tuesday September 6th 1825.

Round times varied. Remarks: Dist 1. George Kay sick on Sept 5th; and on Sept 6th, reports that between 9-11 o'clock it was very noisy with people returning from Gorton Market.

Wednesday morning, September 7th 1825.

Remarks: John Mark brought to the lock-up at half past ten o'clock by Mrs Hardie and Mr Thomas Chantler on a charge of stealing a shuttle. He was discharged on Sept 8th by Mr Etholdstone.

Thursday morning, September 8th 1825.

Notes confirm round times varied. At eleven o'clock, the under mentioned men were taken to lock-up in custody for fighting at the Blacksmith's Arms. George Lowe, John Young and Robert Kenott. At twelve o'clock, Mary McLennan brought to the lock-ups as a vagrant and for being disorderly on the Ashton Road.

Remarks: Discharged - gave £4. £3 to be distributed to the poor of Ardwick and one for damages. Discharged on Sept 8th by order of Mr Etholdstone.

Monday morning, September 12th 1825.

Dist 5. John Royle and Supt William Heywood and I visited the watchmen on the under mentioned hours. Other round times also varied. 1st round, half past nine to a quarter past twelve.

Henry Vaudrey reports when going his ten o'clock round, he found Joshua Oldfield of Hooley Hill, very much in liquor. He stated that he had been drinking at Mr Gee's and that he had been stripped of his small clothing, a hat and pair of shoes and he might have had ten or eleven shillings taken from him by some man who stopped his mouth. He could not describe the person. Remarks: He was brought to the office and kept till morning.

Henry Vaudrey reports that on going his three o'clock round, a number of boards were on fire that had been placed against a brick kiln on Ashton Road. He threw them down and extinguished the fire.

Wednesday morning, September 14th 1825.

Round times varied. Remarks: Henry Vaudrey reports that at half past nine o'clock some person attempted to draw some handkerchiefs through the cotter hole of Mr Renshaw's shop on Ashton Road but was alarmed and made off with parts of two.

Sunday morning, September 18th 1825.

Round times varied. Remarks: At one o'clock, William Haywood brought Thomas Yates to the lock-up for making a disturbance and beating his wife. He was discharged on Sept 19th.

Wednesday morning, September 21st 1825.

Remarks: George Kay in liquor going on duty at nine o'clock.

Thursday morning September 22nd until Friday September 30th 1825.

Round times varied. No reports.

[Final comments from James Wood senior. Most future reports signed by Thomas Chantler.]

Sunday morning, October 9th 1825.

Dist 5. Remarks: William Heywood asleep in his box from eleven till twelve o'clock; and the following day, October 10th; Dist 6, he noted John Wood was not on his rounds from one till four o'clock.

Saturday morning, October 15th 1825.

Dist 6. Remarks: William Williams found two men on a brick kiln in Ashton Lane and took them into custody.

Sunday morning, October 23rd 1825.

Dist 6. William Williams not on his rounds from one till four o'clock.

Monday morning, October 24th 1825.

Dist 6. William Heywood found one man on a brick kiln in Ashton Road and took him into custody.

Friday morning, October 28th 1825.

Dist 3. Robert Carter sent his coat down at five past nine o'clock; the following day, Saturday, he was reported off-duty.

Sunday morning, October 30th 1825.

Dist 3. Carter off-duty.

Dist 5. Royle sent his coat down by five past nine o'clock.

Dist 6. Mr Heywood says that on going his two o'clock round he saw two men running down Pin Mill Brow. Soon after, he found that an attempt had been made to get into Wilf Ainsworth's kitchen window in Ashton Lane.

Monday morning, October 31st 1825.

Dist 2. Smith found James Beswick drunk and without a hat on the Green.

Friday morning, November 4th 1825.

Dist 2. One lamp out at half past nine o'clock.

Dist 3. Two lamps out at by the Green.

Dist 3. One lamp out at Union Street corner.

Saturday morning, November 5th 1825.

Dist 5. Mr Hardy interfered improperly with Royle the watchman while in the discharge of his duty.

Sunday morning, November 6th 1825.

Dist 3. One lamp out at the end of Union Street. Broken by the wind, it being cradled before.

Monday morning, November 7th 1825.

Dist 1. One lamp next to Fothersal's on the Green.

Dist 2. One lamp out on Chapel Street.

Reports then switch from morning to evenings but were still signed by Thomas Chantler.

Tuesday evening, November 8th 1825.

Dist 3. Three lamps out next to Mr Kennedy's on the Green.

Dist 4. Two lamps out at the Polygon and Mrs Wilson's.

Wednesday evening, November 9th 1825.

Dist 1. One lamp out on the Green.

Dist 6. Two lamps on Cotter Lane in Renshaw's shop window on Ashton Lane.

Thursday evening, November 10th 1825.

Dist 1. Lamp out at the Dinnington's.

Dist 2. Lamp out at Chapel on the Green.

Dist 3. Lamp out at Bremner's.

Dist 4. Lamps out. One at end of Hyde Road and one at Polygon.

No reports from 10–22 May 1825.

Wednesday evening, May 23rd 1825.

Dist 19. Lamps were put up in Ashton Lane, Dark Lane and Hallows Lane.

Dist 6. One lamp broke by a cart in Ashton Lane while it lay on the ground.

Friday evening, November 25th 1825.

Dist 6. Samuel Young struck Vaudrey the watchman while on his duty. Mr Chantler ordered a warrant and had Young taken before magistrates and fined 14 shillings.

Sunday evening, November 27th 1825.

Dist 6. Vaudrey saw some men going into Mr Sale's hayloft and informed him. On going towards the loft he became alarmed from someone saying the men had threatened to shoot anyone that came near. Upon which, he 'ricked' and came to me.

When I got there, I found four Ardwick and one Chorlton Row watchmen in Mr Sale's house and Mr Sale serving them drink. I told him they should not do it. I found that the men who had been in the loft were now in the kitchen with a quart of ale before them.

I asked the landlord if he had any charge against them, he said the watchmen made a great stir about nothing. I desired all to go about their business. When we got into the office, Smith the watchman was with Henry Vaudrey. I told him he had better hold his tongue in the street and said if he had anything to say, he should speak in a proper place.

He replied he would speak where he liked. He did not care a damn for any man. Remarks: One lamp broken by Mr Renshaw's cows in Ashton Lane, which he paid for.

No reports from 28 November – 1 December 1825.

Friday evening, December 2nd 1825.

A great many lamps out being on a windy night.

Saturday evening, December 3rd 1825.

Dist 4. One lamp out near Mrs Marshall's between nine and ten o'clock.

Sunday evening, December 4th 1825.

Dist 4. Marshall's lamp out.

Dist 3. Lamp out at end of Hyde Road.

Dist 2. Window loose at Mr Duckray.

Monday evening, December 5th 1825.

One lamp broken at corner of Bingon's works and lamplighter said it was broken before and blamed the frost.

Dist 4. One lamp out at Mass Hall.

Dist 5. One lamp out at corner of Duck Lane.

No reports from 5–14 December 1825.

Thursday morning, December 15th 1825.

Dist 1. One lamp out at Medlock Street.

Dist 2. Two lamps out end of Chapel Street and one at Isaac Gardens.

Dist 3. Eight lamps out from Ardwick Terrace to Chancery Lane.

Dist 4. One lamp out at Polygon.

Dist 5. One lamp out at Brick Street, 3 at Ashton Lane.

Dist 6. Two lamps out at Riverside.

Remarks; Another windy evening.

Friday, December 16th 1825.

Dist 5. Toll House, Shutter Lane at five o'clock.

Saturday, December 17th 1825.

Dist 5. Playing of cards at General Brick at half past twelve on Sunday morning.

Tuesday morning, December 20th 1825.

Dist 5. At half past one this morning, five men were disorderly and were spoken to by Mr Vaudrey after which they ill-used him, Heywood and Royle got him away from them.

Monday January 2nd 1826.

Dist 5. Watchman Royle off sick.

Dist 6. Vaudrey off and Heywood did their duty. About three o'clock on Tuesday morning, three men came over the edge in Ashton Lane and knocked Grundy down and kicked him, and said if he had been the watchman they would have killed him.

Tuesday January 3rd 1826.

Dist 2. One lamp on Chapel Street and one at Marriott Street.

Dist 5. Two lamps on Ashton Lane.

Wednesday January 4th 1826.

Dist 3. Four lamps out. Two at corner of Chapel Street; one at Mr Buchan's and one at Union Street.

Dist 4. Lamp missing from Stockport Road and found top of Mr Preston's wall. Lamplighter said it was broken.

Thursday January 5th 1826.

Dist 1. Three lamps out. Two at Tipping Street and one at Grove Street.

Dist 2. One lamp out at the Green and one at Manor Street.

Dist 3. Two lamps out at Union Street.

Friday January 6th 1826.

Dist 6. McGee's window uncottered. And John Gee's barrow left out.

Saturday January 7th 1826.

Dist 5. Royle says that at three o'clock this morning, three men came over a gate in Ashton Lane and told him if they did not give it him there, they would before long. He disposes they were part of the same gang that had ill-used him before.

Thursday January 26th 1826.

Dist 5. Mr Renshaw's window shutters loose.

Friday January 27th 1826.

Dist 5. Royle says company was turned out of Mr Sales at half past two this morning.

Sunday February 5th 1826.

Dist 5. Royle reports he found the butcher's shop in Ashton Lane broken into.

March 23rd 1826.

Dist 2. Bridge's shop window shutters loose.

March 24th 1826.

Dist 6. Three cotters loose at Gee's.

Dist 5. One loose at Gilbert's and one at Foster's.

March 25th 1826.

Dist 3. Mr Longdon's back door open.

Dist 2. Mr Yates's front door open.

April 1st 1826.

Dist 2. Mr Chapman's window open. Mr Hoult's washroom window open.

September 1st 1826.

Dist 5. Thomas Smethurst taken from Gillibrand's shop and brought to lock-up as he broke through wall.

September 3rd 1826.

Dist 1. Jones says that about one o'clock in the morning, he heard a noise and went to Mrs Butterworth in Downing Street and found the windows taken out but nothing taken away.

Sunday morning, December 31st 1826.

Dist 5. Royle absent from his round from one o'clock.

Dist 3. Mr Heywood absent from one o'clock and without returning this morning.

Tuesday morning, June 19th 1827.

Dist 1. William Jones in liquor when coming off duty.

Tuesday morning, June 26th 1827.

Dist 1. William Jones in liquor when coming off duty.

Sunday morning, November 4th 1827.

Districts 5, 4 and 2. Royle, Heywood and George Grimshaw in liquor at two o'clock in the morning. Heywood missed much of his round from two till

five o'clock and left his lantern upon Mr Oliver's shop.
Sunday morning, November 11th 1827.
    Dist 4. William Heywood in liquor when coming off duty and missed his
round between two and five o'clock.

No further entries or reports until April 1828. Most were still signed by Thomas
Chantler although Alsibrook Sampson signed one entry in report book dated
12 August 1831.

April 19th 1828.
    Dist 1. Mr Longden states that the watchman of No I round is in the habit
of enticing their watchdog off the premises
Thursday morning, April 24th 1828.
    Dist 1. Jones absent from his round from three till four o'clock.
April 2nd 1830.
    Dist 1. Henry Vaudrey says that he has had direction from Mr Berry in
Tipping Street to inform him that when their gates were open, and in telling
the servants on Thursday night when going his ten o'clock rounds, he was
told they would shut it when they were ready.

The following reports appear at the back of watch book and are signed by
Richard Nicholson. They run from 10 April–18 May 1830.

Saturday night, April 10th 1830.
    District 1. Henry Vaudrey brought a woman Mr Duckworth named, Mary
Fleming, to lock-up – not appearing, all charged with assaulting, Mr Foster.
Discharged Duckworth and created a great hue at New Bailey, noise was
about the printers turnout on the 12th at his works at ten o'clock.
    District 3. James Smith says that Shelmerdin, back of Club Row, about ten
o'clock, was drunk and insulting his wife, but on his going up, he went in
the house and was quiet – and also J. H. Cocker, Chancery Lane, about one
o'clock was drunk and very riotous but he persuaded him to be quiet and
he went home.
    He also said a quantity of men were at the back of Mr Gregg's house ferret
hunting all night and he disturbed them about three o'clock.
    District 6. Thomas Gardner & John Royle dispersed a fight at Gillibrands at
20 minutes past one – they came out of Gillibrands to fight.
    Richard Nicholson.

Sunday night, April 11th 1830.

Dist 5. John Royle absent.

Dist 1. Henry Vaudrey reports that Gaskin's house window shuts were open when he went on his 10 o'clock rounds.

Monday night, 12th April 1830.

Dist 3. James Smith absent.

Dist 6. Thomas Gardner reports that Pete Murphy followed him down Pin Mill Brow and struck him behind the neck, he 'ricked' and Murphy ran away making a great noise.

Dist 1. Vaudrey found Hollingworth's yard gate open at ten o'clock and he called them up to fasten it. Mr Cooke's back-sash loose at ten and he told them and when he went again at eleven & twelve it was the same. He told them again & they fastened it

Dist 3. The supernumerary John Donegan, upon going passed Jones's house in John's Street, set his dog at him, and Smith says he is always conducting himself very ill and creating a great disturbance.

Tuesday night, 13th April 1830.

Dist 3. James Smith reports having found the windows open at No 20 Union Street and no one in the house at ten o'clock and it was eleven before they came in that he could inform them.

Dist 1. Vaudrey found the butcher's window open next to Watson's in Tipping Street and had to knock them up.

Wednesday night, 14th April 1830.

Dist 1. About 2 o'clock Vaudrey found the coal grid lifted up at No 3 next to Holbrook's in Tipping Street and he knocked them up to secure it.

Dist 6. Gardner at ten o'clock found Gee's coalhole door open and he enlisted Mr Gee to secure it.

Friday night, 16th April 1830.

Grimshaw reports that as he and Barnes were going from the office at nine o'clock they met with a man near Mr Willet's house very drunk and upon moving him, his hat dropped off and a bladder which contained whiskey came out of it and they examined him and found a measure supposed to be used in selling it off. Nothing else being found they let him go and assisted him on the Stockport cart. The bladder and measure all remain at the office.

Saturday night, 17th April 1830.

George Grimshaw was suddenly taken ill on his 11 o'clock rounds. He found Mr Kennedy's back door unbolted after that he was so far bad that he could not go on his rounds and Donegan the supernumerary was sent on his rounds. No report.

Thursday night, 22nd April 1830.

Dist 6. Thomas Gardner found on going on his ten o'clock rounds that Mr Gee's back window shutter with a cotter and he told them and at twelve they took no notice.

Dist 5. John Royle found Mrs Owens's pawnshop windows unfastened at ten o'clock and he informed them of it.

Friday night, April 23rd 1830.

Dist 6. Gardner again found Gee's back window shutter without cotter and he informed them at ten and eleven o'clock, when Mr Gee said they had forgot to get a cotter.

Dist 3. James Smith found Browne's door open at ten o'clock – and them all gone to bed.

Saturday night, 24th April 1830.

Dist 1. Henry Vaudrey reports that at two o'clock he heard a 'rick' in Water Street, Charlton Rows, he went and found there had been a fight. He assisted to take the persons to the Chorlton Rows police office where the captain of the Watch took 2/6 each as security for their appearance at New Bailey on Monday.

Dist 5. Royal reports that on going his 9 o'clock round he heard of watch in William Street, upon going, he found that it was Mr Kenyon calling who stated that he had been attacked by five or six men who took his hat and his spectacles. His hat was found soon after by a neighbour. He states that at eleven o'clock he heard a cry of 'murder' in Ashton Road. He went up and found a woman apparently drunk and her basket with its contents scattered on the ground, which caused him to miss part of his eleven o'clock round.

Sunday night, 25th April 1830.

Dist 4. I visited the watchman several times during the night and at twelve o'clock I found that Joshua Barnes was not attending to his duty and I stopped on his round. It was nearly five o'clock that he came about half drunk. I spoke to him about it, when he at first denied being off at ale but he eventually said that he hoped I would not say anything, but he had been at Mr Lees in the Polygon knocking them up at three o'clock. I was informed by a Chorlton Row watchman that he had heard him at that time but although I looked for him diligently, I could neither trace by inquiry, nor find anything of him.

Tuesday night, 27th April 1830.

Dist 6. Gardner found Gee's door open at half past one o-clock. They were all gone to bed and he knocked them up.

Dist 1. Vaudrey found Mr Woods door open at ten o'clock. He was a long time before he could make them hear and at last was answered from the Garrett.

Wednesday night, 28th April 1830.

Dist 2. Grimshaw found Mr Bunting's window in Paddock Street and he awoke them.

Thursday night, 29th April 1830. No reports.

Friday night, 30th April 1830.

Dist 1. Vaudrey found a window open at eleven o'clock next to Gaskin's and nobody in the house. It was fastened when he saw it again.

Saturday night, 1st May 1830.

Dist 6. Thomas Gardner was absent.

Dist 2. Grimshaw found Mr Birch's dining room window open at eleven o'clock and he wakened them to fasten it.

Sunday night, 2nd May 1830.

Dist 5. Royle reports that one night this week in Ashton Road, some person threw a heavy stone at him, which hit him on one of his legs. He looked but could not find anyone, and this night another stone was thrown at him but did not hit him and he supposes they are the same parties, which threw on both nights.

Monday night, 3rd May 1830.

Dist 6. Gardner says Gee's coalhole door still remaining open although he repeatedly told them and any person may go through the beer house or yard.

Tuesday night, 4th May 1830.

Dist 5. Royle reports that at ten o'clock Roe's window shutter was open – on his ten o'clock rounds in Ashton Road, near the General Brick, he met the waiter and another man near the front door. The waiter began to take him with him. He then began to tie the shutters and behind the watering stone he found a ham. He took it with him into the General Brick and asked the landlord if he knew he owned the ham and they went to search the kitchen where they found one more missing. The landlord directed him to search the company and the room but could not find the missing one. He left the ham with the landlord. The company he searched were in the snug and he knew them to be of bad character.

Dist 3. Smith reports that ongoing his twelve o'clock rounds, he was talking with Mr Hewitt at his door when a man came to ask whether Hewitt had lent anybody his handcart. He said he had not. The man went back and

Thomas Ireland followed him and overtook the men with the handcart near the top of the Green when they said they had borrowed it knowing different, but he let them go and kept the cart. Smith also following thinking it was suspicious circumstances but did not get near enough to them to either see them or hear what occurred suspecting the matter. Through this, Smith missed his twelve o'clock round.

Saturday night, May 8th 1830.

Dist 3. James Smith reports that Parish in Moulds Buildings was creating a great noise about two o'clock in the morning and insulting his wife shamefully. He could do no good with him and he was obliged to bring him to the lock-up – and his wife promised to appear against him. Through this, Vaudrey, who came to Smith's assistance when he 'ricked' him. He and Smith, missed part of their two o'clock rounds.

Tuesday night, 11th May 1830.

Dist 6. Thomas Gardner absent.

Dist 5. At a house in Sharples Buildings, Royle found open at ten o'clock and at eleven o'clock, he found Prickett's Smithy broken open but nothing missing when he informed them. Royal at twelve o'clock was also called into the General Brick to turn the customers out and when he went at one o'clock he found them fighting in the road and he dispersed them.

Dist 3. John Caffery was fighting with his wife at 10 o'clock and she cried 'watch' and Smith went out and got them into the house.

Wednesday night, May 12th 1830.

Dist 1. Vaudrey found Mr Booth's distillery of wine door unfastened at eleven o'clock and the shutters too. He informed them of the circumstances when they said they did not know.

Thursday night, May 13th 1830.

Dist 5. John Royle on going his nine o'clock round heard a cry of 'stop thief' and 'murder,' which caused him to run to beside of Barton's factory, where he found two men carrying a chair, a ring and some clothing. They were charged by an old man with stripping his house, where Royle, with the assistance of Mr George Hall, took them into custody.

Having of the occurrence, I overtook them in Union Street, whereupon getting them into the office, I found the old man to be Parish, who was in the lock-ups on Saturday night charged with great cruelty towards his wife and one of the prisoners his son, who was assisting his mother to carry away her things in consequence of the father's repeated ill usage. The clothing consisted of his mother's – and with the exception of the chair and ring, the old man laid no claim – seeing it was a family affair we discharged the man at the office.

At eleven o'clock, Royle found Barker's window shuts and Schofield's back gate open.

Friday night, 14th May 1830.

Dist 3. Smith reports that during the time he was going his two o'clock round he found that two lamp tops had been taken off in Chancery Lane by some person. He awaited but could see no one stirring he looked for the tops and he found them at three o'clock in Cheslett's Field.

Dist 1. Henry Vaudrey reports that at 3 o'clock he found a large bunch of onions hung at Watson's door. He knocked them up to take them in. He said he had received something hanging before but thought it was only a rag or something that way.

Saturday night, 15th May 1830.

Dist 2. George Grimshaw reports that Wilf Yates's back door was open and he desired them to fasten it.

Dist 5. Royle reports that at 12 o'clock he and Gardner were called in to the General Brick to assist in turning some company out who had brought a pack of cards with them and the landlord would not allow them to play and took the cards from them, they kicked up a hue and were rowdy. Mr Gill was obliged at first to get Mr Corns and Mr Taylor, who were in the house to assist him and had it not been for the assistance of the watchmen, Mr Gill and the two constables would have been badly ill used as a mob had congregated and collected a quantity of fellows in the street. This caused Garner & Royle to miss the remainder of the twelve o'clock round.

Dist 3. Smith says that the same party came on his round at one o'clock. They went to the King, and he turned them out as through the night on part of his one o'clock round.

Sunday night, 16th May 1830.

Dist 2. George Grimshaw reports that at nearly one o'clock Wm Heaviside called for him and sent him to search for some person in the house. I went with him and upon getting there, found a woman of the town in Mr H's custody. I searched her, but upon inquiry it turned out that she had been brought into the house by his son James – we of course, sent her about her business. Grimshaw through this, lost part of his one o'clock round.

Dist 1. Vaudrey reports that he found at ten o'clock the house at No 2 Stone Street open, both windows and shutters, and Leake's shop door open.

Tuesday night, 18th May 1830.

Dist 1. Vaudrey reports that he found Boulton's front door open at ten o'clock and everybody gone to bed. He waked them and they got up and had to wake Mr Watson to fasten their window shuts at same time.

August 2nd 1831.

Dist 4. Joshua Barnes off his rounds from half past one till half past three.

Dist 5. John Ryley off his rounds from two till four o'clock. He says he was taken very sick at Toll Bar.

Dist 6. Thomas Gardner was off from two till half past three o'clock.

Thursday morning, August 12th 1831.

Barnes was off his round from half past one o'clock till half past three o'clock in the morning. John Ryley from two till four o'clock; and Thomas Gardner from two till half past three o'clock.

James Wood, Thomas Chantler or Richard Nicholson completed most entries during this initial period in the record book - and Alsibrook Sampson made the final entry of that section.

Saturday night, August 20th 1831.

Dist 4. Joshua Barnes absent. Calling his twelve o'clock round at half past one.

Friday morning, August 26th 1831.

Dist 6. Thomas Gardner and John Ryley seen coming from the King public house in Chancery Lane with Sarah Moorcroft at a quarter to one. Landlady refused to file them drink.

Saturday August 27th 1831.

Sandy Cheetham, Mr Steele's coachman threatened to knock Henry Vaudrey down for attempting to stop a foot race at the bottom of the Green.

Wednesday August 31st 1831.

Dist 4. Joshua Barnes. Rev McGibrand's house in Shakespeare Street was broken into and robbed. He complained of neglect on the part of the watchman, not attending to his duty.

On the same night, Mrs Johnson's house at the top of the Green was attempted. The window in the front porch was broken but the entrance was inwards by the inside shutter. The house is included in the Chorlton Row watchman's round, which is taken in lieu of the houses belonging to Chorlton Row on the Ardwick side of the Green - and watched by the Ardwick watchmen.

Tuesday night, 6th September 1831.

Dist 5 & 6. John Ryley and Thomas Gardner report that on Monday night about eleven o'clock, they were called into the George & Dragon public house in Ashton Lane to separate fighting at the house. The landlord ceased filling drinks. The men who had before been upstairs then came down and went back into the taproom and persisted in staying there. Notwithstanding, no drinks were allowed. About one a.m. the watchmen were again called in, and desired to clear the house, as the company would not otherwise go but continued fighting and disturbing the peace. While the watchmen were clearing the house, a bulldog, which belonged to one of the company, flew at Gardner and bit him. In consequence they missed calling on much of their eleven o'clock & one o'clock rounds. Gardner reported to office that the shop door under his alleyway was open all night.

Saturday morning, September 10th 1831.

Dist 3. James Smith's round. Mr Lee found one Saturday morning when putting out the lights, a coat and three loaves. He afterwards discovered that the bake house belonging to Mr Clarke had been broken open and robbed of the above-mentioned articles. He went with Mr Clarke to the baker and Smith, the watchman, in search of the thieves but could hear nothing of them. Mr Clarke's baker found Royle the watchman asleep upon some sheaves. He said when questioned that he was watching the thieves. Smith later said he found two hats and a handkerchief on the opposite side of the road to Mr Clarke's.

Dist 6. Thomas Gardner saw three men from the Lime Works about eleven o'clock. They had been cutting the rope belonging to the Gin. A house was broken open and robbed in Pin Mill Yard of a shirt and some calico.

Dist 2. George Grimshaw. Five men were creating a disturbance by singing and shouting about three o'clock in the morning.

Dist 1. Henry Vaudrey. On Thursday night, the gate and the coach house door belonging to Mr Dawson's house were left open. The watchman locked the coach house doors and returned the key next morning.

Dist 1. Vaudrey. Mrs Dean and lad left the stable door open; the watchman awoke them to fasten it.

Remarks: John Ryley suspended on Sept 10th.

September 18th 1831.

Dist 5. James Smith. Mr Jackson's house in Birch Street was broken open. Theft included a ladies workbox, silk shawl, silver snuffbox, pencil case, bodkin thimble and some rich lace and zip of stiff shoes.

Dist 3. James Smith. On Sunday, a fight in Symes Place about twelve o'clock at night but was dispersed by Sampson, James Smith and George Grimshaw.

Saturday night, September 24th 1831.

Dist 2. George Grimshaw about eleven o'clock found some cloth in Mr Farrington's yard and no one around it.

Thursday October 6th 1831.

Dist 6. A fight broke out in a stable belonging to John Hebden in Pin Mill Yard. The watchmen, except Hooley, were detained to guard the property until nearly four o'clock.

Thursday October 13th 1831.

Dist 2. George Grimshaw found Mr Howard's window shutter open about twelve o'clock.

Saturday night, October 15th 1831.

Dist 1. Thomas Gardner found Mr Duckworth's print shop window open in Stone Street.

Sunday night, October 16th 1831.

Dist 2. George Grimshaw found Mr Agnew's front window open on his ten o'clock round. The same night he found Mr Newbury's window half open.

Monday night, October 24th 1831.

Dist 4. James Woolley found Mr Henry McConnell's garden door open at about eleven o'clock.

Saturday night, October 29th 1831.

Dist 3. John Dollaghan found Mrs Crowley's front door open about twelve o'clock.

Dist 1. T.Gardner. Found on Saturday night near Manor Street, upon the Green, a bonnet and an umbrella.

November 14th 1831.

Dist 2. George Grimshaw found Mrs Mawson's window shuts open at about eleven o'clock. On November 18th, he found Mr Birch's dining room window open.

December 5th 1831.

Dist 1. Thomas Gardner found two men at the bottom of Mr EP Thompson's cellar. They knocked him down before he was aware and then ran away – he sprang to his 'rick' and Smith came to his assistance but upon examination all were found correct. Mr Thompson later sent up to say his shipping had been robbed.

December 22nd 1831.

George Grimshaw found Mr Mawson's window shutters open.

January 24th 1832.

Thomas Gardner and George Grimshaw said that a stone was thrown at Mr Thorpe's window in Manor Street. The following day, Grimshaw found Mr Agnew's and Mr Bateman's back doors open.

February 4th 1832.

Dist 2. George Grimshaw found Mr Birch's dining room window open. He also found Mr Bird's cellar window open all night. He hailed the servant but he did not make it.

March 19th 1832.

Dist 6. Woolley found two foals in Mr Townsend's plant at Polygon at half past one o'clock in the morning.

April 3rd 1832.

Dist 6. Samuel Woolley found drunk on his eleven o'clock round by Joseph Grimshaw and William Ashton and he was ordered to be suspended and that Thomas Harrop be appointed in his place.

April 6th 1832.

Dist 2. George Grimshaw's watch box was burnt down at half past twelve o'clock on Friday morning while he was going his round.

April 17th 1832.

Dist 1. Thomas Gardner found Henry Heaton kicking at William Bradshaw's door and he said that he wanted some more beer. When Mr Bradshaw opened, he tried to knock him down. He would not fill him any more at two o'clock in the morning.

May 10th 1832.

Dist 2. George Grimshaw found Mr Crimson's back door open at eleven o'clock rounds.

May 18th 1832.

Dist 2. John Hewitt's shop was broken open at a quarter before ten o'clock at night and four sheep were stolen.

May 21st 1832.

Dist 2. George Grimshaw found Mr Hewitt's stable door unlocked at two o'clock in the morning.

June 14th 1832.

Dist 2. George Grimshaw reports that Cheetham Steel's coachman and Hall, a joiner, were fighting on Monday night about four o'clock.

June 15th 1832.

Dist 1. Thomas Gardner found William Toplin's shop door broken into about eleven o'clock at night. Mr Gardner went with him and when he came out he said nothing was stolen.

June 22nd 1832.

Dist 1. George Grimshaw found Mr Slack's warehouse door open at ten o'clock.

Dist 2. James Smith missed part of his twelve o'clock round through a riot raised by two men and two women at Mr Gee through being refused lodgings.

June 28th 1832.

Dist 3. John Dollaghan found a man's hat at Summer Place owned by Robert Clarke.

July 7th 1832.

Dist 6. John Parry found three men at Mr Barker's brick kiln.

July 10th 1832.

Dist 5. James Smith found four men at Lime Kiln at three o'clock in the morning.

July 16th 1832.

Dist 1. George Grimshaw found Mr Leatherbarrow's window shuts loose.

July 24th 1832.

Dist 2. Thomas Gardner found Mr Barlow's window open.

July 25th 1832.

Dist 2. Thomas Gardner found Mr Schofield's parlour window not made fast.

July 28th 1832.

Dist 4. James Foster found three men very drunk in Shakespeare Street.

August 4th 1832.

Dist 3. John Dollaghan found Robert Ransom very ill drunk at Mrs Shaw's door and he said that he had been robbed of his watch by three men about a quarter of an hour before.

August 10th 1832.

Dist 6. John Andrews found some men fighting at Mr Gee's door about eleven o'clock at night.

August 14th 1832.

Dist 5. John Parry found a man in Ashton Road and he saw that he was knocked down and robbed of four shillings by four men who ran away.

August 17th 1832.

Dist 4. James Foster says he was going his eleven o'clock round that a man with white hawse and blue jacket got over Mr Watkins's wall into the grounds and opened the kitchen window and then went into the garden and ran away.

August 20th 1832.

Dist 1. George Grimshaw says that he found Mr Leak's window not made at eleven o'clock.

August 25th 1832.

Dist 6. John Andrews says that four men and two women were fighting at the end of Chancery Lane and that he called John Parry for assistance and got them away.

September 4th 1832.

Dist 2. Thomas Gardner found John Hewitt's stable door open at three o'clock in the morning and he went to call them up.

September 10th 1832.

Dist 2. Thomas Gardner found Mr Toplis's blacksmith shop door open at half past 2 in the morning.

September 20th 1832.

Dist 2. Thomas Gardner says that Mr Jones was knocked down and abused.

September 24th 1832.

Dist 3. John Dollaghan says that he was charged by William Murray to assist him to take Ralph Bradley for stealing his hat and that he was brought to the lock-up and sent to the New Bailey.

September 28th 1832.

Dist 3. John Dollaghan brought William Williamson to the lock-ups for striking him on his duty.

October 17th 1832.

Dist 6. John Andrews found John Hebden's mill door open on his two o'clock rounds.

October 24th 1832.

Dist 5. John Parry found Mr George Shatwell's parlour window open on his twelve o'clock rounds.

October 27th 1832.

Dist 4. James Foster found Mr J. B. Clarke's parlour window open.

November 11th 1832.

Dist 2. Thomas Gardner says that he found liquor very nearly out of Mr Thomas Fletcher's parlour window on his twelve o'clock rounds.

Monday November 12th 1832.

Dist 1. George Grimshaw found Mr Duckworth's print works window open at twelve o'clock.

Wednesday November 14th 1832.

Dist 1. George Grimshaw found Mr John Higginton's butcher shop window not made fast on his eleven o'clock rounds.

Wednesday November 15th 1832.

Dist 5. John Parry found John Hewitt's house door open on his twelve o'clock round and them all in bed.

Sunday morning, November 18th 1832.

Dist 3. About 2 o'clock. John Dollaghan found Mr Walker's and Moscrap joiners shop on fire - and it was burnt down.

Monday November 19th 1832.

Dist 1. George Grimshaw found Mrs Holmes garden door open on his eleven o'clock round and Mr Slack's warehouse door open on the same round.

Monday night, November 19th 1832.

Dist 4. James Foster found two very bad looking men lurking about on his round about one o'clock. He watched them for a long time and they went on the Stockport Road.

Tuesday night, November 27th 1832.

Dist 2. Thomas Gardner found Mr PF Williams's gates and coach house door open on his eleven o'clock round.

Dist 5. John Parry found Mrs Walker's house door open at twelve o'clock.

Wednesday night, November 28th 1832.

Dist 1. George Grimshaw found Mr Kay's coal grate open on his twelve o'clock round.

Wednesday December 5th 1832.

Dist 4. James Foster said that he heard something in Mr John Barnes garden as if somebody was breaking open a door when. Mr Barnes said that two men had just gone out of the garden they found open the window shuts.

Thursday night, December 20th 1832.

Dist 3. John Dollaghan found Mr Armstrong's window shuts open at half past ten o'clock.

Wednesday December 26th 1832.

Dist 1. Thomas Gardner found J Tipping's smithy door open at eleven o'clock. Same night, John Hewitt's sheep pen open and sheep out at half past eleven o'clock.

Sunday January 6th 1833.

James Foster says that he found four windows open at Mr Schuster's home about eleven o'clock.

Monday January 7th 1833.

John Parry found Joseph Hardy's window shutter open on his eleven o'clock round and them in bed, he called them up to wake them.

Thursday January 17th 1833.

George Grimshaw found Mr S. H. Slack warehouse shutters open on his ten & eleven o'clock rounds and said they made a practise [sic] of leaving them open.

Friday January 18th 1833.

John Dollaghan found John Crowther's window open at half past eleven o'clock.

Saturday January 19th 1833.

Robert Kenyon suspended for being very drunk when coming off his patrol at nine o'clock and Edward McCann appointed on his round at the meeting.

Sunday morning, January 20th 1833.

John Parry says that Mr Brierley had about 80 lbs of beef and mutton stolen from his lobby in the yard and a single barrel gun from the Garding house. John Andrews says that he found Mr Gee's window open about two o'clock and his wheelbarrow in the street.

Tuesday January 22nd 1833.

John Parry suspended for being drunk rescuing a person from the constable of Openshaw on the 21st January 1833; and Robert Waite appointed on his round on the meeting night.

February 22nd 1833.

John Dollaghan found George Young trying John Clarke's window shutter and door about two o'clock in the morning. He brought him to the lock-up and went to New Bailey. He was committed for 14 days.

February 26th 1833.

George Grimshaw found Mr Duckworth's stable door open on his eleven o'clock round and Mr Leatherbarrow's window cotters loose on the same round.

February 28th 1833.

George Grimshaw found Mr William Wadsworth's back door open at about eleven o'clock and them all in bed.

Monday morning, March 4th 1833.

Thomas Gardner saw a fire at Mr Johnson's new house in Hyde Road about three o'clock and was got out with little damage.

March 8th 1833.

George Grimshaw reports that he found Mr Higginton's shop open at eleven o'clock and them all in bed.

March 10th 1833.

John Dollaghan found Mr Knight's window open at ten o'clock and them all in bed.

March 11th 1833.

John Andrews found John Hewitt's shop door open and them asleep. At eleven o'clock. James Foster found John Wilkinson's window shuts open. George Grimshaw found Mr Duckworth's window shuts open on his eleven o'clock round.

March 12th 1833.

George Grimshaw found Mr Hack's back door open on his twelve o'clock round.

March 14th 1833.

Thomas Gardner found John Hewitt's slaughterhouse window broken open and four calf feet at the outside door on his five o'clock round.

Saturday March 23rd 1833.

George Grimshaw found all John Leatherbarrow's window shutters unfastened about two o'clock in the morning.

Friday March 29th 1833.

Thomas Gardner charged Robert Walton with tricking him on his eleven o'clock round and he was brought to the lock-ups.

Sunday March 31st 1833.

George Grimshaw says that he saw William Oliver's paper mill on fire about 5 o'clock in the morning and that he gave alarm to the Manchester watchmen.

Wednesday April 3rd 1833.

John Andrew found in Hyde Road a sociable and horse thrown over and the horse first and the coachman lying injured at some distance off. They belonged to William Robinson of Stockport. The man was so drunk when they brought him to the lock-up that he could not speak.

Tuesday April 23rd 1833.

Thomas Gardner found John Hewitt's coach hose door open about one o'clock in the morning.

Saturday April 27th 1833.

Thomas Gardner found John Hewitt's coach house door open on his two o'clock round.

Monday April 29th 1833.

George Grimshaw found Mr Isherwood's front door open and them all in bed on his eleven o'clock round.

Tuesday April 30th 1833.

Thomas Pimblott found the counting house open at Lime works on his ten o'clock round. Same night, James Foster found Mr William Clowes window shuts open on his eleven o'clock round.

Tuesday May 7th 1833.

John Dollaghan found Mr Armstrong's front window open and he told the servant of it. The same night, James Foster found Mr Schuster's window open and he told the servant but he did not shut them. Same night, Mr Slack's window was open.

Saturday May 7th 1833.

John Andrews said that there was fighting at Joseph Shaw at eleven o'clock and him and Pimblott went in to turn them out. Same night, John Andrew found William Renshaw's shop window shutter open on his twelve o'clock round.

Same night, Thomas Gardner found Mr Bargele's new house open with a quantity of lead in it and he went to Mr Egan to tell him and he came to lock the door.

Saturday June 20th, 1833.

James Foster reports that seven men stopped Mr Richard Dearman and robbed him of his watch.

Sunday morning, June 30th 1833.

Thomas Pimblott brought Henry Eaton to the lock-up for assaulting and abusing John Steel of Openshaw.

Thursday July 18th 1833.

George Grimshaw found Mr John Higginson's back yard door open about twelve o'clock. Same night, he found John Higginson's slaughterhouse door open about one o'clock - but nothing was missing.

Monday morning, July 29th 1833.

Thomas Pimblott and some brick makers found three horses and game. No account of them at the office but was drunk all day with the brick makers and came at night to the office very drunk to go on his duty. I was told that he was very drunk and that he should not go on and he said that he would go on and thus was not drunk. I suspended him till the next morning and put William Smith on his round.

Tuesday July 30th 1833.

James Foster says a person came to him from Stockport and said that he had been robbed of some clothing last night.

Thomas Gardner brought a man to the office with a bundle because he would not give an account of it. When he was at the office, he gave several different accounts of it. At last he saw that his name was William Howard and that he lives at No 4 Briton Street, Bank Top.

That was the final entry in the old watch book.

2. Robert Peel and the First Policing System

Robert Peel was a dedicated, and highly controversial legal reformer, who as Home Secretary, carried out an urgent review of the criminal code and a massive shake-up of the country's existing policing system.

Born at Chamber Hall, Bury in Lancashire on 5 February 1788, Peel was the third child and eldest son of Sir Robert Peel, the MP for Tamworth, a very wealthy mill owner, who also ran a local spinning and print works. Robert junior endured a very strict upbringing, having to remember and twice repeat the Sunday sermon. He was a brilliant scholar, attending Harrow School and Christ Church College, Oxford, winning a double first in both classics and mathematics. It was always his ambition to follow in his father's footsteps and become an Member of Parliament and in 1809, aged just twenty-one, as a reward for his academic success, his father purchased for him the small rural seat of Cashell, in County Tipperary, which had only twenty-four voters. Just three years later, Peel exchanged it for a more prestigious constituency at Chippenham.

Young Peel made an immediate impact in politics, and when he first addressed the House of Commons, the Speaker, Charles Abbott, declared: 'That was the best speech since that of William Pitt'. A year later, the Duke of Portland, appointed Peel as Under Secretary of State for War & the Colonies. Working under Lord Liverpool, he helped to reorganise the militia in readiness for any threat from the French. After Lord Liverpool became Prime Minister, Peel was appointed the Chief Secretary for Ireland in May 1812.

Peel attempted to end corruption in public office, but in 1814, he almost lost his life when he challenged his bitter rival Daniel O'Connell to a duel at Ostende in Belgium, following a row over plans to suppress the Catholic Board. Fortunately for Peel, O'Connell was arrested en-route.

In 1817, Peel decided to retire from the post of Chief Secretary, a decision which upset many Irish Protestants who signed a petition to try and persuade him to stay. Oxford University finally recognised his services to Protestantism and invited him to become their very own MP in 1822. He later rejoined Lord Liverpool's government as Home Secretary.

Still in his early thirties, Peel then spent much of next five years preparing urgent reforms of both the legal system and the gaols. He reduced the number of offences that automatically carried a death sentence, and helped to repeal more than 250 old statutes.

In February 1827, Lord Liverpool was suddenly taken ill with paralysis,and was replaced as Prime Minister by George Canning. Peel however, severely opposed Canning's religious policies and beliefs and immediately resigned. He returned to office again the following year when his close friend, the Duke of Wellington, took over the leadership of the party, and re-appointed him Home Secretary.

The introduction of his Metropolitan Police Act in 1829, had an immediate effect upon policing in London; and although his policies were later adopted nationwide, at first, they led to mixed emotions and some drastic action from a sceptical public. For some time, Peel and Wellington received death threats and became worried about city reprisals – due to the rapid implementation of their severe measures. Peel however, realised that, in the eighty years or so since Henry Fielding had adopted similar reforms and introduced the Bow Street Runners, public demand for law and order had changed and there was now a unique opportunity to co-ordinate all forms of policing including a radical review of the Thames police, horse patrols, foot patrols, parish constables and watchmen, and he also confirmed plans to create a specialised detective office.

One of his proposals was establish a new force to help keep the peace. At this period in London, crime was again rampant and Peel claimed he had only had a few hundred men to patrol the streets, and just eight magistrates, each responsible for about eight to twelve runners. The existing system was, he said, ineffective and inefficient and he demanded all sections be incorporated within one new organisation of unarmed, paid and fully equipped police under the control of two Commissioners of Police.

Peel announced a 'Nine Points of Law' plan: This was to be an integral part of his proposed Police Bill. They included:

• The basic mission for which the police exist is to prevent crime and disorder.

• The ability of the police to perform their duties is dependent upon public approval of police actions.

• Police must secure the willing co-operation of the public in voluntary observance of the law to be able to secure and maintain the respect of the public.

• The degree of co-operation of the public that can be secured diminishes proportionately to the necessity of the use of physical force.

• Police seek and preserve public favour not by catering to public opinion but by constantly demonstrating absolute impartial service to the law.

• Police use physical force to the extent necessary to secure observance of the law or to restore order only when the exercise of persuasion, advice and warning is found to be insufficient.

• Police, at all times, should maintain a relationship with the public that gives reality to the historic tradition that the police are the public and the public are the police; the police being only members of the public who are paid to give full-time attention to duties which are incumbent on every citizen in the interests of community welfare and existence.

• Police should always direct their action strictly towards their functions and never appear to usurp the powers of the judiciary.

• The test of police efficiency is the absence of crime and disorder, not the visible evidence of police action in dealing with it.

The Metropolitan Police Act

Peel's new Metropolitan Police Bill was passed on 19 July 1829. And on 29 September, less than two months after the Bill was adopted, his first batch of one thousand men were turned out from Whitehall - in a great long line – for publicity purposes to begin patrolling the streets of London.

Peel celebrated his success with the appointment of two new Police Commissioners, who supervised the massive re-organisation. They included ex-Army officer, Colonel Charles Rowan, and a young barrister, Richard Mayne.

This newly created Metropolitan Police Force only patrolled the London districts, whilst the rest of the country continued much as before with existing policing methods, and in most cases, it was another decade before other authorities introduced their own police forces.

The new London policemen were called 'Bobbies' or 'Peelers' after their founder and their new uniform included top hats and blue tailcoats. This colour distinguished them from red-coated soldiers, and scarlet waistcoats of the famous Bow Street Runners.

Officers were required to wear their uniforms at all times – both on and off duty, to avoid any potential claims of spying. They also carried rattles and were armed with wooden truncheons. They only received a guinea a week and were allowed just five unpaid days holiday per year.

Many policemen, particularly in rural areas were desperately short of money and kept livestock to help supplement their income. Some even kept guinea fowl in their station houses but first had to request permission from police headquarters.

Most worked in long shifts and were not allowed to vote in any elections. They even had to seek permission to marry. Church attendance too was considered part of their duties and in most areas, officers had to attend a monthly 'Pay Parade' to claim their wages. It was an unusual tradition that continued for another eighty years!

Despite Peel's pledge that his new force were better trained, better turned out, more efficient and paid, they were certainly not very popular at first with the general public.

And it took another decade before the 'Peelers' were finally accepted. The tide seemed to turn following the murder of a young policemen in Holborn, when residents saddened by such a vicious and unprovoked attack, organised a collection for the man's widow and family.

Many authorities nationwide, waited as long as possible before establishing their own forces, and to a certain extent, most waited until they were forced to adopt these radical measures by the introduction of the Municipal Corporation Act in 1835. This ruling insisted that all Borough's and Cities outside London should create their own police forces.

A Model Force
The Peelers eventually became the model for all forces and in some regions, a few Chief Constables were appointed from senior London officers, or by experienced Army officers with extensive military experience.

In Manchester, many forces came into operation when towns were first incorporated. This involved the election of councillors, then raising the rates to help pay for the force, and finally a Watch Committee to supervise the officers.

It was nearly ten years after the Police Act before Manchester and districts formed their own force but by 1899, all suburban areas had their own systems.

Lancashire and Cheshire Constabularies covered some suburban towns and yet ironically, one town that decided not to have its own force was Bury, the former hometown of Peel! Bury opted to come under the jurisdiction of the Lancashire force, and remained so until 1974!

Robert Peel died on July 2nd 1850, following injuries sustained from a fall from his horse a few days earlier on Constitution Hill. He was sixty-two years old. Despite a love-hate relationship with both fellow politicians and the public, the nation mourned for him, and Bury built a rather grand statue to his memory.

Following public subscription, the town also constructed Peel Tower at the top of nearby Holcombe Hill, so that theoretically he could still keep watch over the town, and the rest of the Manchester area.

Scotland Yard and the Criminal Investigation Department

Following Peel's extensive overhaul of the Metropolitan police system, he soon set about re-organising and re-locating his detectives to new offices within a centralised location, and took a very keen interest in scientific research.

Initially, he transferred his team of investigators from Bow Street to an old 18th century building within a large area known as Scotland Yards.' It seemed a bold move to leave Bow Street, and their established police headquarters – and the venue for the Metropolitan Magistrates Court – where most of London's important criminal trials were heard, yet once again Peel triumphed.

The first move included use of the old Market police office in Whitehall Gardens, which had previously been used for Army recruitment purposes. And in 1843, the first specialised Criminal Investigation Department (CID) was created.

This was an entirely separate force and consisted of an Inspector and six Constables, who were all dressed in plain clothing! They were primarily appointed to help deal with a specific new threat termed 'Terrorism,' and related to potential attacks from foreign agents, and from a new Irish-based splinter group, known as the 'Dynamiters,' who had begun a series of devastating bombing attacks against prominent targets.

During this period, the country also faced major immigration problems with an influx of unwanted refugees from revolutionary countries.

The detective team also worked closely with a specialised unit at the Post Office Science Crime Laboratory, established in Bell Yard, near Temple Bar. Their brief was to help counter a new scientific war that had developed since the introduction of the penny post, and now involved potential risk from parcel and letter bombs.

By 1850, surprisingly, the detective offices had outgrown this location and offices were hastily constructed at Great Scotland Yard, with the Metropolitan Police HQ in one section, and the public carriage licensing offices in another.

This building though and others became the subject of bombing attacks by terrorist groups, who once exploded a powerful device that practically destroyed the detective office.

Fortunately, it was unoccupied at the time but the explosion demolished a nearby pub, packed with other off-duty policemen, and several members of the public.

Many were badly injured by the blast – two seriously. This proved to be a very lucky escape for the detectives, who over the next few years also had to deal with many other unexpected and similar incidents in the London region.

In 1886, there were massive explosions at both Paddington and Victoria Stations in the heart of the City, and another smaller incident at Ludgate Hill. The attacks continued intermittently, and other notable targets later included large private houses, rail and road bridges, trains, public buildings and even ancient monuments.

One major similar incident of note was an attack on Nelson's Column in Trafalgar Square, on 30 May 1894. Records indicate the police were members of a newly formed anti-terrorist squad, who had been summoned about 9.20pm.

The danger apparently came from an unexploded and highly unpredictable package, consisting of sixteen cakes of dynamite –

already fused – and tied to the foot of the Column. Fortunately, this proved to be one of the few times attackers failed to detonate a device, and the slight delay allowed officers to dismantle the bomb.

This incident though, provided a stark wake up call to the Government, who revised their efforts to try and counter any future attacks and began to employ specialist police officers with military backgrounds and explosives experience.

The Metropolitan Police Headquarters moved on several occasions. The latest seemed to be about 1890, when they relocated to new Scotland Yard offices, situated off Derby Street, close to Whitehall.

At this site, they were finally able to boast about having their own crime laboratory and began to deal with the advance of photographic reproduction and witnessed the birth of fingerprinting, and the introduction of an extensive criminal records system.

False Uniforms

In early 1894, and shortly before the Nelson's Column incident, the authorities expressed concern over certain individuals fraudulently wearing false military style uniforms. Many were said to be disgruntled ex-soldiers, or down and out civilians, who could regularly be seen begging on the streets and abusing the Queen's uniform.

The Government, worried about 'Trojan Horse' style terrorist attacks, and the need to clean up the city streets, quickly introduced the Uniforms Act, which made it a punishable offence for any civilian to wear service apparel, in part or total, or any dress designed to imitate any service uniform.

This new Act also covered the unauthorised wearing of military medals, orders and rank badges. In addition, it also endorsed an instruction given to police officers that they had to wear their uniforms at all times to confirm their role within the community.

This period saw the introduction of the extensive use of photography ('Mug Shots') to record the faces and details of criminals and the scenes of crimes. Fingerprinting techniques were also developed and introduced at Scotland Yard in 1901.

3. Detective Superintendent Jerome Caminada

Jerome Caminada was said to be one of Manchester's most successful thief-takers. A former engineer, born of mixed race parentage, with an Irish mother and an Italian father, he joined the city's police force in February 1868 — and enjoyed a highly successful thirty-one year career, becoming the first Superintendent of Detectives. My great grandfather worked with him on many occasions over several years until Caminada retired in 1899. James served under him, first as a detective constable, then as a detective sergeant. They were based in the same office.

Caminada was born in the very poor Deansgate area of the city in 1844. His father, Francesco, came to England from the Lombardy region of Italy during a time of political unrest in his home country. He was just one of many thousands who took a similar journey seeking a peaceful life, with new opportunities for their families. Bizarrely, many settled in the Ancoats area – which quickly gained the nickname of 'Little Italy' where, despite exchanging the lush rolling hills and mountains of their native lands for the dark, satanic mills, and tall dirty black, smoke-stacks and belching chimneys of east Manchester, many immigrants saw this a vast improvement to their earlier basic way of life. Most moved into one-hundred year old former mill houses, which although needing extensive renovation and repairs to protect against the cold winter weather, still offered exceptional accommodation with living rooms, bedrooms and outside toilets.

The Italian immigrants soon introduced Catholic Whit Walks and homemade ice-cream to the city, and gradually began to import other specialist food products from their native regions and helped establish a unique and highly successful business empire. These new settlers, however, did not always have everything their own way, and from the initial arrivals in 1865, until the latter immigrants of around 1900, often clashed with rival English and Irish inhabitants and neighbours. Fortunately, this 'Little Italy' soon established its own identity, and

Jerome Caminada.

quickly brought welcome colour, vitality and prosperity to the area.

Caminada was a staunch Roman Catholic and was just twenty-four years old when he first joined the Manchester force as a constable. At that time, the police were only about eight-hundred strong, and had to deal with a population of 350,000.

On his first night of duty, Caminada, had to deal with an incident of a serious wounding; where a well-known local drunkard, known as Fat Martha, was attacked and stabbed in the stomach. First he had to help sober her up before she could be treated. This was of course, at a time long before any emergency services, and he soon realised that it was part of a policeman's lot to care for the sick and injured and take them if necessary, to the nearest infirmary. In some cases, this meant a hike of several miles aided by fellow officers, and carrying the casualty on a handcart or stretcher.

Three years after joining the force, he gained promotion to sergeant and was introduced to the newly created Detectives' Office where he gained an enviable reputation as an exceptional 'thief-taker,' claiming several cash awards for the successful detection, arrest and subsequent conviction of many dangerous and habitual criminals.

Caminada was said to have imprisoned 1,125 people during his career, for a whole variety of crimes. He worked with a vast network of informants, and it was said he met many at his local St Mary's Church in Mulberry Street. He was a rough, tough and often ruthless individual, who was extremely ambitious and was afraid of nothing and no one. He became much feared within the criminal fraternity and established a mean reputation for being able to defend himself, and was never concerned about using his fists, a gun or any other weapon, in order to secure the arrest of a supposedly dangerous villain.

In 1888, he was promoted again, this time to detective inspector and helped introduce the use of photography and 'mug-shots' to help catch and deter criminals.

He was known as a master of disguise and sometimes acted undercover to secure arrests and convictions. He once hid in a piano case; and on another occasion posed as a patient to expose a quack doctor. His powers of detection became legendary following an investigation into a mysterious Hackney carriage murder. In trying to establish whether the victim had been deliberately drugged or poisoned before being robbed, he persuaded the surgeon to send away an organ from the victim for scientific testing in the new crime laboratory. He later caught the killer at home with some of the victim's possessions.

Despite his bullish attitude, Caminada bizarrely tried to help the families of criminals that he had put away and was determined to tackle many social issues, including trying to addess the problems of re-offenders.

He received many worrying threats and attacks during service and one experienced villain, Robert Horridge, vowed he would kill him. The man fired two shots at fellow officers in an effort to escape justice, but Caminada tracked him down, and used his pistol to make the arrest.

Caminada and many other detectives carried firearms. He had cause to use his own gun on numerous occasions. His personal favourite was a Colt .38 calibre double-action revolver, made from blue steel, with a chequered walnut handle. Other guns were supplied through the Army at Pall Mall, London, and most were made of nickel or chromium plated to prevent rust. James had his own Army service revolver and I understand that due to his military experience, he was allowed use of this as and when required. He also gave instruction to other officers in the use of firearms.

In addition to crime investigation, Caminada also took a tough stance on the unlawful sale of alcohol and lewd entertainment. He claimed to have helped to close over four hundred public and beer houses around the city. He prosecuted many landlords for selling illegal ale, or serving customers cheaper poisonous substitutes.

He retired from the police force in 1899, and the supervisory Manchester Watch Committee rewarded him with a 'handsome pension'. In later years, he worked as an estate agent, and private investigator before taking an interest in local politics, becoming a city councillor.

Records indicate that unfortunately, Jerome Caminada enjoyed less than fifteen years of retirement. He was apparently involved in a road traffic accident in north Wales sometime during 1913, and later died from the results of his injuries the following year at his home in Moss Side. He was seventy years of age.

In 1895, and just a few years before his retirement, Caminada published the first of two comprehensive volumes about his work with the Manchester Police. It was entitled *Twenty Five Years of Detective Life*, and published by John Heywood of Deansgate & Ridgefield, Manchester. He dedicated the book to the Chief Constable, Charles Malcolm Wood. In the Preface to the first volume he surprisingly made a general criticism against the few fictional crime writers of the day, claiming:

> Unlike so many so-called stories of detectives, these are founded on facts, and are from first to last, in all their details truthful histories of the crimes they purport to describe, and of the detectives and punishment to the criminals.

He explained the work consisted of fifty stories dealing with all manner of crime and criminals. He stated:

> The methods of quack doctors are exposed and the credulity of their victims revealed; the practices of swindlers and impostors of all kinds laid bare, including exploiters of sham registry offices, bogus agencies of various kinds, next of kin frauds, insurance and other swindles, begging letter writers are exposed and the modus operandi of burglars, pickpockets, watch snatchers, racecourse thieves etc, are described and dealt with.

He added:

In compiling the experiences, I have guarded myself against giving to individual's unnecessary offence or pain. I have endeavoured also, when dealing occasionally with subjects of a delicate or risky nature, to do so in language free from offence that may be read alike by old and young of both sexes.

He also explained that, at the time when he joined the police force, the area and character of what he called 'Criminal Manchester,' was very different from what it was then (1895). Both sides of Deansgate, then a narrow street or lane fringed with property of the lowest class, were hotbeds of crime. The widening of Deansgate, the early closing of public houses and the building of Central Station did much to break up the Deansgate colony, whilst a better supervision of the police tended to keep down crime in other parts of the city. He also claimed within his introduction:

That Manchester with all its great moral, religious and political associations, its commercial enterprise recognised in every part of the world, and its corresponding wealth, still has its dark spots.

'Within an arrow's flight of the princely grandeur of the Town Hall may be seen many dreary dwellings of misery and wretchedness.

'Twenty-seven years ago however, things were much worse! Then in

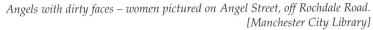

Angels with dirty faces – women pictured on Angel Street, off Rochdale Road.
[Manchester City Library]

Charter Street and Angel Meadow, not so much of a meadow now, and in the vicious streets around to which my thoughts are at the same time directed, "the wicked never ceased from troubling, nor were the weary ever at rest," for the fitful midnight slumbers gave place, as daylight broke, to the restlessness of evil.

Caminada gave a highly graphic and most vivid description of life on the dark, dangerous city streets and within the grotesque slums of Manchester from 1868 onwards, claiming:

The exterior of one of theses houses to which I propose to carry the mind of the reader will be a fair specimen of the rest. It present a dingy face of crumbling brick, begrimed by the soot of years.

The elevation consists of three storeys; the first two are lighted by windows which denote unmistakable antiquity, and multifarious are the methods employed to refuse wind and rain admittance.

Tattered garments, crowns of old hats, brown paper, and paper rendered brown by exposure, are all pressed into the service of stopping a hole; and so varied are the contrivances utilised for this purpose, that the several windows are more suggestive of a rag merchant's establishment than a dwelling house of Christian England in the 19th century.

On entering, we proceed along a lobby until we come to a room whence issues a babel of tongues, and in which a scene as extraordinary as can be conceived presents itself. The apartment is full of men and women, though the former predominate.

Some are seated on broken backed chairs, or upon dilapidated stools ranged round a filthy table, most of the occupants eagerly devouring various kinds of messes, washed down by tea, coffee or beer. Others again, are on their knees before the fire – one broiling a red herring; another a slice of fat bacon.

Some appear to have just left their beds, or, as is more probable, being obliged to quit them, have descended to the common room in a state of dishabille, and are proceeding to attach their tattered rags to their persons in the best way they can.

Some of the women are patching garments, the primitive colour of which has long since vanished; others are endeavouring to make a stocking perform its duty one day more. And crouched on each side of the fire, such as it is, sit two thinly clad creatures, whose bruised and disfigured faces are eloquent examples of the "bully's" brutal treatment, which many of Eve's fallen and forlorn daughters have to endure.

Running along one side of the room is a dirty bench on which a large number of men are smoking and drinking. The furniture is of the most meagre description, and consists of one table, some half-dozen broken backed chairs, two stools and a bench.

The walls are dotted with gaudily coloured prints, the subjects of which are mostly of a licentious nature. A few common ornaments are on the mantelpiece, the principal one being a large blue earthenware dog with a brown tail. The room reeks; the whole scene is squalid and cheerless; yet no sense of shame is visible on the countenances of the motley occupants.

The ribaldry of one black-browed fellow is equalled only by the dreadful oaths of the young girl by his side, and the grossness of the mere child is applauded by a hoary-headed wretch whose condemnatory substantives are the familiar flowers of his speech.

Then look at the object of pity, once a bright-eyed girl, on whose lap lies an infant with scarcely a shred to cover its delicate little form. One cannot help wondering what sort of life is in store for this blameless infant. A happy one it cannot be. For what chance will it have in future years of escaping the sinful surroundings of its birth?

Let the reader still follow me in imagination to view the scene upstairs. The passages are narrow, the plaster broken in many places, the stairs weak and yielding to our footsteps. The room we enter contains four dirty rickety beds, mere pallets, the threadbare and ragged covering of which fails to conceal the creaking bedsteads and dirty straw mattresses beneath.

The boards of the floor seem to have had no contact with the scrubbing brush for years, and we note the absence of all arrangements for personal cleanliness. On those beds rest, or rather restlessly lie, men and women of various types and ages, from the frowning confirmed felon to the innocent bastard babe.

There lie old and young - grey headed convict, wizened wig, infant and child of tender years – presenting a sickening picture of moral depravity; the atmosphere being nothing but a foetid composition of pestilential vapour emitted from filthy beds, dirty clothing, foul breath, and worse than all, the presence of offensive matter in the room.

Before we enter, out step is heard upon the stairs, and the wretches, who have learned from experience the necessity of watchfulness, are awake and on the alert. The word 'D's' detectives runs around the room as

Poverty and wealth merge on the streets of Victorian Manchester.
[Manchester City Library]

we enter and commence to inspect the inmates of the different beds.

'Now then! Sit up! Let's look at your phizzogs!' and men, women and children instantly obey, passive as lambs, with the remark, 'Oh, is it you Mr Jerome?'

The inspection over, and none of them being wanted they sink once more into a morbid slumber until the sorrowful daylight enters, and the unhallowed repose gives place to trouble, sin and debauchery.

Doubtless, the sad fate of most of these wretches is attributable to their own persistence in criminal and wayward folly. Yea, they may not only have shaped their own crooked paths, but have willingly paced them until hardened in heart and reckless in consequence.'

Jerome Caminada makes mention of the general behaviour, crimes and activities performed daily by many slum dwellers. He explained:

Occasionally, we come across men, woman and children, who followed no regular callings, and yet were not members of the criminal class, but whose daily familiarity with hideous aspects of crime and debauchery, with fallen women and professional thieves, could scarcely fail in their ultimate evil effects, especially when honest work became scarce.

The occupants of such houses chiefly graduated from 'snow-droppers' (strippers of clothes lines), to 'cracksmen' (burglars), and fallen women.

The latter were often seen parading along Market Street in their characteristic blue gowns and jacket make-up of factory lasses.

On some of the principal thoroughfares at midday, we find the sham 'sailors' and 'colliers' begging along the streets with legs and arms professedly crippled, and although they had never been to sea, or down a coal mine, drawling out in doleful voice. Fearful tales of shipwreck and coal mine explosions; and of their miraculous escapes from death with the loss of an arm or leg.

Visit them in their lodgings, or in their well known beer house rendezvous and you would find they can use their disabled limbs in a very nimble manner.

Another class of impostors, that I might call 'land sharks', street tradesmen in a small way, known also as 'dry land sailors'. They could be seen parading Shudehill or lounging at street corners, or in public houses in quest of their prey.

The majority of their victims were country rustics whom they plausibly decoyed into some quiet back street or alleyway, under the pretence they had some smuggled articles, which they could sell them very cheap.

They usually consisted of remnants of cloth, or silk, and sometimes tobacco, or cigars, all of them damaged goods, and purchased from another tradesman, but by wearing the typical sailor dress and chewing tobacco in seaman fashion, they found little difficulty in disposing of their wares at twice or three times their value to unsuspecting simpletons.

Caminada went on to describe certain other parts of the city that were notorious for specialised crimes. He again emphasised the neighbourhood of Deansgate and claimed this was the rendezvous of thieves and a hotbed of social iniquity and vice. He confirmed:

The women of the locality were of the most degraded class, and their chief victims were drunken men, collier lads and country 'flats' whom they picked up and rifled with impunity.

Wood Street, Spinning Field, Hardman Street, Dolefield and the adjacent courts and alleys on the one side, and Fleet Street, Lombard Street, Lad Lane and Bootle Street on the other side of Deansgate, were the worst haunts of vice.

Such places as the Dog & Rat, the Red, White & Blue, the Old Ship, the Pat McCarthy, and the Green Man, and other notorious places, were then in full swing as licensed beer houses. Passing along, the pedestrian's ear would be arrested by the sound of music proceeding from mechanical organs, accompanied sometime by drums or tambourines. On entering, you would find a number of youths and girls assembled in a room furnished with a few wooden forms and tables.

The women generally lived upon the premises, the proprietor of the den adding to his income by the proceeds of their shame. Some rude attempt would be made to sing at an indecent song by a half drunken girl for the edification of some collier lads, who were the chief victims of these haunts, but her voice would be drowned by the incessant quarrelling and obscene language of her companions.

He confirmed that many of these places had no licence whatever for the sale of intoxicating liquors, and explained there were other well known beer houses which did nearly all their trade during prohibited hours – selling all sorts of poisonous stuff to the public under the guise of beer and spirits.

Deansgate was also a noted place for prize fighting. In several of the garrets there were regular rings of stakes and ropes. When the battles were stopped, the fights took place in kitchens, stables, cellars, or in any other place the police were not likely to put in an appearance. Many of the garrets were also fitted up for dog fights and drawing the badger and 'Swells', who did not mind paying for the spectacle used to turn up, sometimes through their own misfortune of losing a watch or another article of value.

Exchange Railway Station. [Manchester City Library]

Other areas of particular concern for the police in Victorian times included the neighbourhoods of Canal Street, Minshull Street, Richmond Street and back of Piccadilly. The detective agreed:

These plague spots were terrible agencies for recruiting year by year the ranks of dangerous society from our middle class population, and many a clerk and other respectable young men have begun their a criminal career by becoming a secret pilferer from the till to obtain the means of gratifying his appetite in such haunts of sin.

Caminada also highlighted the role of 'bullies' or 'coshers' who preyed upon the community. They managed to grab some girl and compelled her to lead a loose life, and when she had accosted and decoyed her victim to some convenient place, allowed the 'cosher' to rob him of all the valuables he possessed and gave numerous other examples of common crime.

He also made bizarre reference to some common punishments, including a 'healthy flogging' and 'birching' of a first offender. Caminada confirmed the facts from such cases of note, stating:

One of Her Majesty's Judges of Assize in a case of robbery with violence, at the trial of prisoners charged with the offence, and who were found guilty by the jury, proceeded to pass sentence.

He informed the prisoners, who were aged from sixteen to twenty years of age, that they were charged with a very serious offence and very properly were found guilty by the jury. Also to send them to penal servitude would be considerable expense to the community.

As they had applied great violence to the prosecutor, he would only give them a short sentence of a few months imprisonment, but each would receive twenty lashes of the cat-o'-nine-tails. The gang referred to were similar to the Manchester Scuttlers.

Caminada added: 'That after lash no 5, I have never known a case where prisoners have come for a second dose of this sort.'

A boy was charged with stealing postage stamps and money from the drawer of a till in the cashier's office of the place where he was employed.

After being detected, he was sentenced by the Stipendiary Magistrate

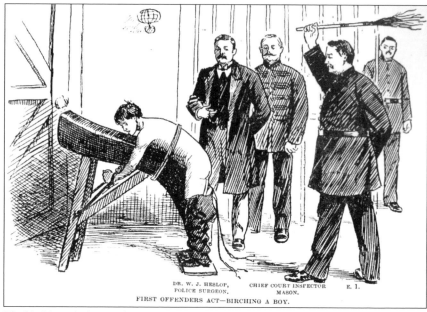

DR. W. J. HESLOP,
POLICE SURGEON.

CHIEF COURT INSPECTOR
MASON.

E. 1.

FIRST OFFENDERS ACT—BIRCHING A BOY.

The birching of a boy as shown in Caminada's autobiography.

to receive twelve strokes with the birch rod. Before a juvenile is birched, a police surgeon examines him; he is then strapped to the horse, his wrists and ankles are strapped, and a body belt goes over his back.

These preliminaries are worse than the birching. The little fellow, not knowing what will really take place, shouts and screams during the strapping process, making it painful to be within hearing.

The birching itself is not severe, but the effect is very deterrent, and has prevented many juveniles from having to be sent to prison. The police surgeon and a police Inspector had to be present in every case of birching.

Jerome Caminada's second volume was published in his own name from 2, Mount Street, Bernard, Whitworth Park, Manchester, during 1900. This was about a year after his retirement. And, once again, he reported a selection of fascinating true-life accounts of his work, offering a similar number of stories to that of his first volume.

It included amongst many others: – a typical Saturday night in Deansgate; great coal frauds; how insurance companies were robbed; the Fenian Conspiracy; the Cronin Murder; prison mysteries; juvenile criminals; and reports of burglary and arson.

In his second book, he also gave details of a review for the Manchester Police force. He said:

The police force of every large town is regarded generally by the people as a kind of civil army of quiet occupation, a gentle force pertaining to the community for their defence and for co-operation with all the respectable members of it, but never for aggression.

The members of it move about almost unarmed, and are welcomed as the visible embodiments of law and order, confirming the safety and security of all who recognise those chief two elements of social and communal life, and checking the erratic tendencies of those who fail to recognise the advantages of civilisation, and who fret under the restraints and limitations alike of labour and poverty.

The feeling that exists between the police and the people is, undoubtedly, of the most friendly and often confiding nature. By the young folks generally they are looked upon with mingled awe and admiration, and by those of them whose consciences are clear, a sense of safety is enjoyed so long as one remains in sight; they feel within reach of omnipotence.

By children of a larger growth and much riper age they are regarded as men of encyclopaedic knowledge, and as peripatetic directories of the names, addresses, and marked characteristics of all the people resident on their respective beats.

This has recently been attested by the wide acceptance of the assurance, sealed by all the principal music hall authorities, and now almost crystallised into a proverb of the century, that when you are worried by uncertainty, even as to the time, you "only have to ask a policemen."

These remarks may. At a casual glance, appear somewhat wide of the mark, but as a matter of fact, they are concerned with the root of the whole business, and touch the first causes that rendered the formation of what we call the force necessary.

He also made reference to the fact many city police stations were situated very close together. He urged reforms and reviews of the number of officers employed and wondered whether the use of so many stations was really necessary.

He was asked to submit about a dozen reports to the Watch

Committee between 1897–9, and claimed he had demonstrated by hard facts how re-arrangements could be effected, antiquated and useless customs abrogated, small abuses abolished, and surplus men supplied with something to do. He claimed that in most cases the men themselves cordially received his suggestions, which he said were never hidden from the individuals concerned.

He cited that police stations at Park Place, Knott Mill, Albert Street, and the Town Hall were just a few hundred yards apart from each other; as were the Police Courts to Fairfield St, Fairfield St to Newton St, Newton St to Goulden St. He said additional stations at Lowe St, Cannel St, Brook St, Openshaw, Fairfield St, Police Court and Belle Vue Street were also equally close together. He proposed that if a re-arrangement of the police divisions were made and a central police station formed for each, it would be found that a great reduction of police stations could be effected.

He also claimed that the City Police Courts had access for hundreds of prisoners and yet occupied a most expensive area of ground, and were only to a small extent occupied. He suggested that if they were utilised as a central lock up for prisoners a very great saving could be effected. He claimed this arrangement would enable the Goulden Street police station to be dispensed with and prisoners transferred to the nearest station.

Inside the CID Office.

He believed this arrangement would materially reduce the cost of conveying prisoners from police stations to police courts because only one van would be required, rather than four at that time.

In the conclusion to his second book, Caminada, said he believed:

The intelligent detective agent is not long in discovering that the lines of demarcation between different classes of criminals are most distinctly marked.

And having obtained an intimate acquaintance with the members of such circles, he is not infrequently able to find a clue to a robbery, or other daring offence, the perpetrator of which has apparently left no trace by which he could be inculpated.

Courage and fixed determination must ever be among the most distinguishing characteristics of the detector of crime; and woe to him if he should once show the 'white feather'. I ascribe no small part of the good fortune, which attended me during my long connection with Manchester police to the fact that I always stood my ground, even when confronted by overpowering odds.

At the same time, I declare with equal confidence that I have never taken a mean or cowardly advantage of a prisoner. I have met men as they emerged from gaol, and done my best, by advice and assistance, to encourage their return to the path of honest labour; and have frequently had the pleasure of helping them on that path, by finding the employment their unaided efforts would have failed to obtain.

Two signed copies of the original volumes of Jerome Caminada's work were personally autographed and handed to my great-grandfather in recognition of his assistance and friendship. Following James's death, the books were later handed down to his only daughter Minnie and eventually onto her husband, Thomas Stinton. In later years, they were given to my mother, and their only daughter Doreen. The books have remained within our family archives ever since.

The Manchester Anarchists, a radical group who campaigned for free speech, became unfairly branded by the authorities as 'irresponsible young men'. Normally, they held their meetings at Ardwick Green, and their ranks included large numbers drawn from both working class men and women. They gained a great deal of adverse publicity from Caminada's initial archive recollections of 1899.

Many of the more dramatic events relating to this group appear in police records around September 1893, and include claims that they were responsible for 'criticising and abusing members of the Royal family'. Caminada reported his personal involvement with this group.

No doubt under pressure from government sources, Manchester's Chief Constable, Charles Malcolm Wood, claimed the anarchists were a 'serious nuisance' and demanded his officers put an immediate stop to their activities. He proposed a number of desperate and determined measures, including the infiltration and disruption of their meetings. And he even tried to persuade the group to move from Ardwick Green to another much quieter site at Stevenson Square. This location, however, was considered too remote by the organisers, who demanded that the public should see and hear their controversial proposals. When his offer was refused, and the meetings continued at the original site, the Chief Constable insisted on much tougher, immediate action, ordering his officers to prevent anyone from speaking, claiming they caused an obstruction.

The press reported that on several occasions, police clashed with both demonstrators and supporters, and in one scuffle, when the main speaker was arrested, Detective Caminada admitted breaking his umbrella by attacking the man – and yet claimed compensation for criminal damage!

Many of these so-called anarchists were charged and imprisoned and Caminada's actions, later came back to both haunt and taunt him, when he became the subject of ridicule during a popular music hall song, often used on the thriving national entertainment circuit. Entitled *The Scamp Who Broke His Gamp at Ardwick Green*, this was generally performed to the tune of *The Man Who Broke the Bank at Monte Carlo*, and to a certain extent, allowed this vigorous campaigning group to claim a rather belated moral victory. The lengthy and descriptive verses in the song, and subsequent brutal actions, only tended to highlight the stupidity and ineptitude of the authorities at that time, and their remarkable determination to ban free speech.

4. James Wood — No Ordinary Policeman

James Wood was born in May 1868, within the run-down and poverty-stricken parish of Hulme in Manchester, the son of Job and Agnes Wood. His father was described in early census forms as a 'cellar man', and later as a 'bottle dealer'. The records also suggest that James was christened the following year in the city's cathedral, and that he had three sisters and a younger brother.

His school report declared him to be a 'bright young scholar,' and he left at the age of fourteen to try his hand at a number of varied occupations. At one time, he was a joiner's apprentice, and may have helped his father at some stage in the licensing trade. Realistically, he was only passing time as he had only one true ambition, to join the army as soon as possible, but had a seemingly endless four years to wait. In the meantime, when another, more interesting, temporary opportunity came about, he seized it with both hands, joining the London & North Western Railway Company as a clerk at Victoria Station in Manchester.

Eventually, he reached the age of eighteen, and signed-up for the newly introduced short-service engagement, a period of seven years in the army, and a further five years in the reserves. Joining the 1st Battalion, the Royal Lancaster Regiment as a promising young infantryman, his records confirm that he first attested for the service at Ashton-Under-Lyne on 16 June 1885, when he was just eighteen years and one month old. He was 5' 6" tall, and had grey-coloured eyes and light hair.

Immediately prior to his enlisting, the 1st Battalion had completed a tour of duty in the West Indies with detachments at penal settlements in New South Wales (Australia) and India. Earlier, they had served in the Crimea and helped in the suppression of the Indian Mutiny. They also provided generous support with an expedition to Abyssinia (now Ethiopia) in 1868, and also took part in the famous Zulu War of 1879.

His regiment was known as the 'King's Own' and was one of the

Sergeant James Wood.

oldest units in the British Army, having been raised in 1680, by the Earl of Plymouth, for service in Tangiers. Uniquely, the men wore the 'Lion of England' on their cap badge and were known as 'The Wanderers'. Just four years before James joined, the regiment was granted a new and more permanent base at Bewerham Barracks, near Lancaster. It is clear to see from James's documents, that the opportunity to join such an illustrious company of men must have felt like a dream come true for an enthusiastic young Mancunian.

Army personnel records from that period are extremely fuzzy and, disappointingly, do not provide much detailed information about individual soldiers. Fortunately James's own records paint a more accurate picture and highlight many important facts. It seems that James saw action in parts of South Africa, sometime between 1885 and 1890. Despite the fact these items are more than one hundred years old, many details are perfectly recorded on long lasting parchment or wax paper. They also confirm that Sergeant (N° 1087) James Wood, of the Royal Lancaster Regiment of Infantry, was discharged from the Army Reserve — slightly ahead of schedule — as a consequence of his being appointed a sergeant in Manchester City Police. The records show him to have served five years and thirty-four days in the regular army, and nine-years, two hundred days in the reserves (and cadets). His total service was said to be fourteen-years and two hundred and thirty-four days. His intended place of residence was 69 Rutland Street, Hulme, Manchester.

James Wood's papers recalling him for service from the Army Reserve.

On February 1900, James received papers recalling him for service with the regulars and ordering him to report to the regimental depot. Failure to report and he would 'be liable to be proceeded against. You will bring with you your 'Small book,' your Life Certificate, Identity Certificate, and Parchment Reserve Certificate'. He was advised to take the notice to the nearest post office where he would receive 'the sum of three shillings as an advance of Reserve Pay, to be adjusted when you join'. His transport costs to Lancaster would be covered by a travel warrant. This order was never acted upon, however, as, on 4 February, he was granted his discharge, undoubtedly because, by this time, he was serving as a police officer in Manchester.

Archive records and details of former police personnel, including

Army Form B. 128.

Should this parchment be lost or mislaid no Duplicate of it can be obtained.

PARCHMENT CERTIFICATE of Discharge of No. *1084* (Rank) *Sergeant*

(Name) *James Wood*

1st Bn. *Royal Lancaster* Regiment of *Infantry*

Born in the Parish of *Hulme* near the Town of *Manchester*

in the County of *Lancashire*

Attested at *Ashton u Lyne* on the *16th June* 18 *85*

for the *Royal Lancaster* Regiment, at the Age of *18½* years.

He is discharged in consequence of *promotion to the rank*
of Sergeant of Police.

*Service towards completion of limited engagement	Army *5* yrs., *34* dys.	Medals and Decorations	*– Nil –*
	Reserve *9* yrs., *200* dys.		*2nd Class Certificate*
	Total *14* yrs., *234* dys.		*of education*
	*Service Abroad *7½* yrs., *254* dys.		

(Place) *LANCASTER*   (Signature of Commanding Officer) *Martin ...*
(Date) *4th February 1900*   *Commanding 4th Reg...*

Discharge confirmed at _____

Signature *...*
Commanding 4th Reg...

Date *4th February 1900*

* To be left blank for completion by the confirming authority.

Discharge Papers of Sgt James Wood from the Army Reserve, February 1900.

James's, are retained at the Greater Manchester Police Museum on Newton Street. They verify much of the information contained with his personal papers and this building is a former police station, opened in 1879, where James probably spent some time during his early career – and ironically was also a place Detective Caminada once recommended for closure! Thankfully, many of the original features of the premises have been retained. And visitors are still able to examine the charge office with its bizarrely-shaped polished counter and see the wooden records cabinets and authentic furniture. They can also see the heavily worn indentation in the counter (where the desk sergeant would lean to hear the circumstances of arrest) and examine several old cells and facilities used throughout the Victorian era.

James Wood first joined the Manchester City Police as a young constable on 30 October 1890, more than five years after he had first joined the Army, and just under ten years before he eventually received his final discharge papers, following promotion to sergeant. He was an experienced soldier, and, seemingly, a very brave infantryman who had seen action overseas. He was said to be an excellent shot with a rifle and had worked with a variety of weapons throughout his military service and was accustomed to handling both firearms and explosives. Prior to discharge, he had been promoted to the rank of sergeant and described in the records as a 'popular and reliable soldier.'

The city force was recruiting quite heavily during 1889/90 and particularly welcomed men with military experience, who were accustomed to handling weapons, and able to deal with an assortment of potentially hostile situations. James matched these relevant criteria. The police records confirm that he had grown an inch and a half since first joining the Army at eighteen. Later documents indicate that he continued to grow, eventually reaching 5' 9^1/$_2$".

His initial police record card claims he was single at the time of entry into the police service, but James was actually married by then! His marriage certificate confirms that he had already wed his local sweetheart from Hulme, Miss Letitia Little on 8 March 1890, at the Parish Church of St Michael's in Hulme. James was only twenty-one years of age, and Letitia nineteen. Letitia's father, William Little, was a French polisher.

Despite obvious hardships, this was certainly a time of great promise and opportunity for the young couple and allowed James to finally settle down after many years of military service. It was a new beginning, and he soon decided to dedicate himself to a bright new career as a young policeman and he was to enjoy a relatively short, but extraordinary career; one that most other officers could only dream about.

James and Letitia Wood, with their daughter, Minnie.

James Wood was certainly no ordinary policeman. Anyone researching his career would soon note his remarkable achievements, steady promotions, commendations, awards, rewards and many reports of meritorious service.

April 1899	Reward for meritorious service.
April 1899	Reported for meritorious conduct – diligence.
February 1900	Recommended for promotion to sergeant.
February 1900	Promotion list.
February 1900	Promoted to sergeant.
December 1901	Recommended for reward.
December 1901	Report of meritorious conduct.
October 1902	Reward.
October 1902	Report of meritorious conduct.

He became an established explosives and firearms expert, utilising his varied military experience and was frequently used by the government to review and supervise explosive operations, and to implement and oversee potential matters of national security. It is quite clear that he also helped in the protection of Royalty and other visiting VIPs. And yet, quite bizarrely, much of his career had passed unnoticed for more than a century until these personal boxes of treasured memorabilia came to light.

His military experience was vitally important too whilst patrolling the uncertain streets of Manchester city centre and the suburbs in this dangerous period of change when many inhabitants refused to go out at night, especially alone, for fear of attack and robbery. How little seems to have changed over the past century! Many gentleman of that era also hired private security guards to watch out for their person and property and often carried a weapon of some description about their own person. Even some police officers were armed! Most constables, however, just carried a wooden truncheon for protection but detectives had access to, and often carried, firearms.

January 1903	Recommended for promotion to inspector under the Explosives Act, 1875.
February 1903	Made inspector under the terms of the Explosives Act, 1875.

December 1903 Promoted to inspector.
January 1906 Applied for superintendency.
June 1907 Report requested for police courts.

The Manchester detectives were a much feared and respected team. This specialised unit had developed rapidly over the fifty or so years since their initial introduction but remained in constant danger from potential attacks due to their obvious capabilities and reputation. In the city areas, they were known as 'Ds' and it was said there was an air of expectation and anticipation when detectives suddenly appeared on the scene to begin asking difficult questions. In many slum areas they were often accompanied by a back-up group of constables, and generally worked in pairs. It is not quite clear as to how many wore plain clothes at the time of James's early career, as some detectives worked undercover, or wore a disguise. Additional officers, cleared for the use of firearms, attended incidents with pistols or rifles, and some constables with army training, were often called in support. James was just such a person. He was young, bright and keen. He was also a very ambitious officer who later helped many of his colleagues to understand the use of weaponry, and the need for self-defence. His experience must have proved invaluable. He worked with a number of particular officers and was often paired off with others, whose names also appeared in dispatches, and within shared newspaper reports.

Perhaps it was his basic training as a teenage clerk with the railways, and with the Royal Lancaster's, that caused James to meticulously maintain his own private cuttings book with photographs and fascinating details of many of the major incidents that he was involved with throughout his police career from 1890–1914. In addition, he also kept many copies of letters, memos and any other relevant paperwork relating to his actions, which have proved extremely useful in trying to piece together precise career achievements.

At the time of his marriage (1890) his address was shown as 27 Dearden Street, Manchester. However, in August 1899, the records show that Detective James Wood lived over a china shop at 69 Rutland Street, Hulme, the same address that was shown on his paperwork on joining the Army in 1885.

James Wood gained several rapid promotions following his initial

The City Police Courts, Minshull Street. [Greater Manchester Police Museum]

period of training and probation, quickly moving from a fully-fledged constable to sergeant, detective sergeant, inspector, detective inspector, chief inspector and, finally, superintendent. He worked in all departments of the service – and especially enjoyed his time in the detectives' office, helping to solve numerous crimes, catching and convicting a host of notorious north-west villains.

At the turn of the twentieth century, his military and policing skills were utilised to maximum effect, helping to organise feasibility studies for special events, and numerous VIP visits to the city. He was also asked to submit other key reports to the Chief Constable on a number of other important matters, including royal visits.

Many promotions were preceded by use of a temporary rank as an 'acting' officer, and with some postings, often took twelve months or more, before official confirmation took place. The following information has been taken directly from James's prized personal files and paperwork, and from other official documents currently held at the Greater Manchester Police Museum. Additional information was collated from newspaper archives and by records held at the Manchester City Library. It should be noted however, that the personnel records do not always contain a full account of all the promotions or case histories, but do confirm a substantial number of rewards and recommendations received during service.

What follow are examples of the many varied and fascinating cases he worked on during his twenty-four year police career. The first cutting dates from August 1898 and relates to one of the fastest arrests and convictions recorded at that time in the Manchester City force. The other cases highlighted, together with copies of supporting paperwork and archive material, provide a unique insight into the workings of the police and about life in general in the city during an incredible period of change, and quite remarkably all have remained locked away within family papers for generations.

25 August 1898
JEWELLERY ROBBERY IN MANCHESTER
A smart arrest

A daring jewellery robbery has been committed in Manchester, and the city police have affected a smart arrest.

This morning about one o'clock the window of Messrs W and F Terry, jewellers of Victoria Street, was smashed from top to bottom and five silver watches were taken.

Information reached the police and efforts were at once made to arrest the culprit. The case was placed in the hands of Detective Sergeants Wood and Jakeman, who, some little time after the robbery, came across a young man named Thomas Halstead, of no fixed address, resting on the forms on the Infirmary Esplanade.

He was bleeding profusely from a wound to the wrist and was accused of having broken into Messrs Terry's shop. He was taken to the Town Hall, and when acquainted with the charge that would be preferred against him, admitted that he was the offender. The watches have been recovered.

THE CULPRIT IN THE DOCK
At the City Police Court this morning, before Mr Headlam, City Stipendiary, Thomas H. Alstead, a slim young fellow of about 19-years of age, was charged in custody with having broken into the premises of William & Frank Terry jewellers, of 8 Victoria Street, in this city, and stolen

eight silver watches valued at £25 from the window.

The story of his arrest provided a very good illustration of the ingenuity and expedition of the city police methods of detection.

Sergeant Wood, who first gave evidence, stated that he, and Sergeant Jakeman, who were on special duty in the neighbourhood, was informed by Constable Harrington soon after one o'clock this morning of the occurrence.

On going there, they found the window (which is valued at about £25) was smashed, and a heavy file was lying inside. Two pieces of broken glass were stained with blood. A tray containing the eight watches was missing. At a subsequent period they obtained from one of the carters employed by the Evening Chronicle, a description of a man whom he had seen running away from the direction of the shop.

The two officers adjourned to the Infirmary Esplanade, where they made a survey of the somnolent occupants of the seats. They examined the hands of each person, and at last came across the prisoner, who had a newly made cut on his wrist.

That was at 5.15am and even then, the cut, which they presumed had been caused by the broken window, was bleeding. Sergeant Jakeman put his hand in the prisoner's trouser pocket and pulled out three of the watches. They charged him with breaking into the shop and stealing the watches, and he replied: 'The game's up, I did it!'

In the meantime, Constable Harrington found two of the watches between the window and an outer covering, and two others on the footpath in the vicinity. Corroborative evidence was given by several other witnesses.

The prisoner was committed to take his trial at the next Sessions.

An undated case from around the same period.

THEFT FROM A SHOP DOOR

This morning at the City Police Court before Mr J Buckley and other magistrates, John Kerr of Rumford Street, Salford, and Harry Escott of Bloom Street, Salford, were charged with stealing two pairs of boots from the shop of Mr Walter Beardow, Stretford Road, Hulme.

Detective Wood was passing along Stretford Road the other evening when he noticed a pair of boots showing under Kerr's coat. The two men were together and seeing that they were observed, they ran away.

The officer gave chase and subsequently arrested them, and it was then discovered that the boots, of which Kerr had two pairs in his possession, had been stolen from Mr Beardow's shop door a few minutes previously. Escott was sent to gaol for a month, and Kerr for 14 days.

Evening News, 13 February 1899
HIGHWAY ROBBERY OFF DEANSGATE

At the City Police Court this afternoon before Mr F. J. Headlam, Andrew Gunn, labourer, was charged with highway robbery with violence and also with receiving a stolen gold watch, knowing it to have been stolen.

About half past eleven on the night of the 7th of the present month, Duncan McKinley, who lives in Hamilton Street, Old Trafford, was attacked in Severn Street, Deansgate, and robbed of his gold watch and chain, and 45s in cash as he lay on the floor.

Two men have since been committed to the Assizes on the charge of being concerned in the affair, and Gunn, and a number of others were arrested in a lodgings-house in Gartside Street by Detective Sergeants Wood and Woolvern.

They were taken to the Town Hall, and prisoner was then identified by a beer housekeeper as the man who had left a watch with him some time previously. In answer to the charge of highway robbery with violence, prisoner said that he was not there. With regards to the charge of receiving stolen property, he replied that he found the watch.

The prisoner was remanded until tomorrow with a review to his committal to the Assizes.

Follow-up article.

THE HIGHWAY ROBBERIES OFF DEANSGATE

Andrew Gunn, the young labourer, who was yesterday remanded by Mr Headlam on a charge of being concerned in the recent highway robberies in the neighbourhood of Deansgate, was today committed to take his trial with the two men already committed, at the Liverpool Assizes, a woman named Martha Fawcett, of Severn Street, having identified the prisoner as one of three men who robbed Duncan McKinley, of Hamilton Street, Old Trafford. Detectives Wood and Woolvern arrested a prisoner in a lodgings-house at two o'clock on Sunday morning.

Albert Street Police Station. [Greater Manchester Police Museum]

Further notes from his cuttings file confirm: 'Tried at Liverpool Assizes on 23rd February, 1899, found guilty and sentenced to 3 months imprisonment and 20 strokes with the 'Cat.' Ten lashes at each six-week's end.'

March, 1899, E Division.
Rewards to detective officers for extraordinary diligence and activity in the discharge of their duties during the months ending 31 March 1899.

PC Wood, award of 7s. 6d.
Other officers rewarded, included: Chief Inspector Hargreaves £5, Inspectors' Corden, Dutton, Edwards and Watson, rewards of £10 each.
Signed: S. Hargreaves, Chief Inspector.

February 1900.
Recommendation to Sergeant
The sub-committee considered the appointment of Sergeants to fill existing vacancies in the Force. Resolved: That the following Constables be

recommended to the Watch Committee for appointments as Sergeants, viz., PC D203. Taylor; PC Davies; PC Wood and PC Goodwin.

The same report also contained some interesting notes of bravery by other constables and detectives, with a particular mention of a PC Webster who assisted in the rescue of three people trapped in a flooded cellar and shop. The report said that when the officer was alerted, the cellar, surrounded by a window and wall, with a floor falling into the cellar, contained about five feet of water.

The Constable without divesting himself of any clothing at once sprang into the water and at great personal risk rescued a boy as he was about to sink. He carried him to a place of safety and entered the building a second time and rescued a woman and child who were clinging to a floating counter.

With assistance, he got them out and they were taken to a place of safety. Through Grafton's exertions and exposure he was taken seriously ill with cramp and was on the sick list for several days.

The police report confirmed.

PC Webster rescued a youth from drowning who had fallen into the cellar attached to the shop at 371 Hyde Road, and would doubtless have been drowned but for the Constable's exertions.

I have received a number of letters from the neighbourhood speaking very highly of the courageous way in which the Constable acted, and it is the general opinion that there would have been a serious loss of life but for Constable's exertions in getting people out of the shop and other buildings.

It was resolved that the recommendations of the Chief Constable be adopted, viz., that Detective Sergeant Woolvern be granted a reward of £5 and the Watch Committee's Medal for Bravery; that Detective Sergeant Ashton, be granted a reward of £5; that PC 629 George Grafton be granted the Watch Committee's Medal for Bravery; That PC 98 David Webster be granted the Watch Committee's Medal for Bravery. Also that the medals be presented to the Officers named at the first available general parade of the Force.

December 1901, E Division
SPECIAL REPORT OF MERITORIOUS SERVICE

Sir,

I beg to submit for your consideration the under mentioned report, the particulars of which I have fully inquired into, and believe to be substantially correct, and I recommend the parties named in the margin as deserving of reward.

Apprehension: By Sergeant Wood.

Whilst in charge of detective office on 29th May last, Wm Cannon came enquiring for a woman supposed locked-up. He was persuaded to wait until records were searched. The Sergeant, knowing that a woman was in custody on suspicion of larceny then telephoned and obtained assistance of Inspector Woolvern and PC Lea, and from enquiries made, it was found that Cannon had committed a burglary at the house of Mr H. Hill, Rusholme. Jewellery to the value of £10 being stolen – this was afterwards recovered.

He was sent to the Sessions and sentenced to 9 months imprisonment. He had served several terms of imprisonment for shop-breaking etc, including a sentence of 4 years penal servitude in London.

Signed: Philip Corden, Chief Inspector.

24 July 1902, Evening News
ALLEGED THEFT OF JEWELLERY
Owners Wanted

Detective Sergeant Wood and Detective Dorricott, passing along Victoria Street, City, on the 18th inst, observed a man named Charles Thompson, who lives in Drake Street, Strangeways, closely examining a watch he had in his possession.

Questioned as to how he came by it, Thompson said that it belonged to his wife. The officers did not consider the man's answer satisfactory and took him into custody.

Subsequently, when at the Town Hall, a gold ring, chain and pendants, besides the watch were found upon him, and he at once confessed to having stolen them from a house in Dover Street, West Gorton, which was occupied by Elizabeth Wilson, who had missed the goods during her temporary absence.

At the City Police Court this morning, Thompson was sent to the

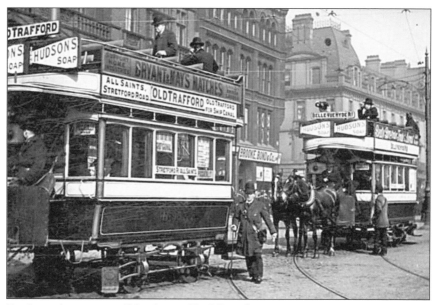

Two horse-drawn trams. [Manchester City Library]

Sessions on a charge of stealing the articles named.

A second charge is about to be preferred against the prisoner of being in possession of stolen goods. When his house was searched on Saturday, the police discovered a quantity of jewellery, which the prisoner says he has found.

The following description of the property has been published:

Gentleman's English Lever, No 28,049, lady's Geneva watch 'The Marvel,' No 280,354, silver and pearl fruit knife, a pair of gold-rimmed spectacles, enamelled half-crown brooch, English penny brooch, floral design on one side with the name of 'Ada' in the centre, silver curb brooch with heart in the centre, lion shilling, ivory handle razor-marked 'one of the best,' a gentleman's blue cloth overcoat with a velvet collar has also been found.

19 October 1902, E Division
SPECIAL REPORT OF MERITORIOUS CONDUCT
Sir,
I beg to submit for your consideration the under mentioned report, the

particulars of which I have fully inquired into, and believe to be substantially correct, and I recommend the parties named in the margin as deserving of reward.

Apprehended on the 18th July 1902, one Charles Thompson, charged under h & a 'jewellery' value £10, proceeds of larceny from dwellings. Committed to Sessions (two cases) sentenced to 9 months.

Remarks: Good strong case. R. Dorricott and Sergeant James Wood given 7s. 6d each reward.

Signed: - Philip Corden, Chief Superintendent.

4 December 1902, *Evening News*
EXTRAORDINARY ALLEGATIONS OF FRAUD
A typewriter agent's stay in Manchester
Some extraordinary allegations of fraud were made at the City Police Court this afternoon. A respectably dressed man named Charles Goad, apparently about 40 years of age, who spoke with a strong American accent, was charged in three instances with obtaining money by false pretences, and in the fourth with embezzlement.

He was apprehended a few days ago by Detective Sergeant Wood in a Blackburn hotel, and before then, he had lived at Liverpool, Blackburn and Manchester.

The charges were of embezzling £11 11s., the moneys of Palmer Howe, Princess Street, obtaining £100 by false pretences from Emma Louise James, Moss Side, under the pretence of supplying Lever Brothers, Port Sunlight, with typewriters; obtaining under similar instances £40 from Walter Seddon, Moss Side, under the pretence of supplying Ogdon's Ltd, with typewriters; and obtaining £80 from Sarkis Taselodjiu under a similar pretence.

With regard to the case in which Mr James prosecuted, it was stated that the prisoner went to her as a lodger in January of this year, and on October 31st he disappeared. During his stay near the end of June he told her, according to her evidence, that he had an order from Levers for a number of second-hand typewriters.

They agreed to share in an undertaking to find the money for twelve machines. Her share was £48 for six machines, and she was to receive in return, £10 for each machine. On the 13th August, he paid her £12, which he said was interest on the £48.

Later, she received a letter from him in the course of which he said he was about to purchase more machines and suggesting that it would be better for her to entrust her money to him and he would yield her a bigger interest than the four or five per cent she was at present getting.

'If you feel you can trust me,' he added. 'I shall be glad to do all I can for you. Assuring you of my desire only to promote my own and your own welfare, yours faithfully, Charles E. Goad.' On the strength of this note, the witness advanced another £52 making in all £100.

Mr Murray: 'So out of the £100 you gave him, you got £12 back?'

'Yes.'

A representative of Messrs Lever, Sunlight Works, Birkenhead, said he did not know the prisoner, and stated emphatically, that the firm did not buy second-hand machines.

In the charge of defrauding Seddon, prosecutor said prisoner represented to him that he had a number of second-hand typewriters which he had obtained for £5, and that he had an order from Messrs Ogdon by which he would make £8 each. On this statement he obtained £40 from Seddon, who was to share in the profits of the transaction.

Prisoner pleaded guilty to these two charges, and the others were not proceeded with.

Inspector Clegg said prisoner had undergone a sentence of twelve months' imprisonment for false pretences, and he had also been in the State Prison, Connecticut, for some offence of which the police did not know the nature.

Detective Sergeant Wood remarked that he had received information that prisoner had received close on £500 in seven or eight cases of a similar character.

Prisoner was sentenced to six months imprisonment in each case and three months in the other — making nine months in all.

1903, *Evening Chronicle*
A BIRMINGHAM TRAVELLER'S LOSS

Mysterious robbery in Manchester

Sidney Aronsberg, jeweller's traveller of Portland Road, Birmingham, brought an action in the Manchester County Court before his Honour Judge Parry this morning, against Mrs Cater, proprietor of the City Hotel, Long Millgate, Manchester, for £4 10s.

Mr Leonard Harris appeared for the plaintiff and Mr J. A. Buckley represented the defendant.

Inside the Manchester Police Court. [Greater Manchester Police Museum]

The plaintiff stated that on the 23rd October last, he travelled from Birmingham in the afternoon and took his baggage to the City Hotel, which was a temperance hotel. His baggage consisted of a skip and two bags, and of the latter contained a purse and the sum of £4 10s., which he put in after he had had his dinner and before he went out.

In the evening, he went to the Queen's Theatre, and when he returned to the hotel, he went into the baggage room and found that the purse was in the bag, but the money had been taken out. The bag at the same time remained locked, as he had locked it, and apparently in the same position in which it had been left.

The plaintiff in reply to Mr Buckley, said he had stayed in the hotel previously and had seen the notices 'The manageress will not be responsible for valuable articles unless given to her personally.'

He went to the pit of the Queen's Theatre after he left the hotel. He could not have had his pocket picked of the amount because it was not in his possession. There was jewellery of the value of £3 and £4 in the bag with the purse and the money, but that was not touched. Asked why he immediately examined the bag when he returned from the theatre, he said he wanted to take his money upstairs.

His Honour remarked that this was a little peculiar proceeding, seeing that he had left the money in the bag during the evening.

In further cross-examination, the plaintiff said that other bags contained jewellery of the value of more than £100. They were not tampered with. He acquainted Miss Cater with his loss as soon as he learned it. The defendant the next morning lent him a sovereign for which he gave her an IOU.

Miss Cater, daughter of the proprietor, stated that she was on duty on the evening referred to, and it would have been scarcely possible for anyone to enter the baggage room and to remain there for a few minutes without her noticing it. The plaintiff remarked to her that the purse must have been left in the bag so as not to incriminate the person who took the money.

Detective Sergeant Wood stated, that he was consulted about the affair, but he failed to trace the money. Answering Mr Harris, the witness said he declined to express an opinion whether there had been a robbery or not. He simply made the usual inquiries.

His Honour spoke of the plaintiff's story as extraordinary. The most likely thing was that he put the purse without the money, into the bag. How he lost the money it was impossible to say, perhaps he had his pocket picked. Judgement would be for the defendant with costs.

CHARGE OF THEFT AND FORGERY

A youth named William Isherwood Eatock, clerk, who lives at Mount Ive, New Lane, Winton and a young man named George Marriott, warehouseman, who lives in Malcolm Square, Coupland Street, Chorlton on Medlock, were charged at the City Police Courts this morning, before the Stipendiary Magistrate, Mr F. J. Headlam, with stealing two cheques, one of the value of £20 and the other £10, and with forging the endorsement of them.

The prisoners were employed by Messrs William Cambell & Sons, rope manufacturers, Cannon Street, and yesterday, they were visited by Detective Sergeants Wood and Ashton and were charged with the offences named, also with uttering the cheques.

A search of the premises was made and the sum of £20 10s. was found under some roping. When the prisoners were being taken to the Town Hall they admitted the offence.

It seemed that the prisoners obtained a couple of blank cheques, which had already been signed by one of the members of the firm. The name of 'E. H. Cambell' was put in as the other signatory and it was endorsed in the same name, which, in the three instances where it occurred, was in the same handwriting.

The bank cashed the cheques, but almost immediately afterwards discovered that the signatures were frauds. Marriott was asked to write the name 'E. H. Cambell' and it was then found that his writing was identical with that on the cheque.

The prisoners were sent to the Assizes for trial.

The case was eventually heard at the Manchester Assizes before Mr Justice Wills.

A MANCHESTER FORGERY CASE

A youth named Wm Isherwood Eatock and George Wm Marriott, pleaded guilty to a charge of having stolen three blank cheques and with having forged two of them for £10 and £20 and cashed them.

Mr Tipping, who conducted the case for the prosecution, said that the prisoners were employed by the firm of Messrs Wm Campbell and Sons of Cannon Street, Manchester, Eatock being a clerk and Marriott a warehouseman.

One member of the firm was an invalid, and in the office were a number of cheques, which bore his signature, as he filled up a number so that they could be used for payment of accounts even when he was not at the office.

The prisoners got hold of three of these cheques, and Marriott filled in the name of another member of the firm on two of them, and cashed them. The fraud was discovered through the bank clerk having his suspicions aroused by the signature, which had been placed on one cheque by Marriott.

When the prisoners were arrested, the sum of £20 was found in a cellar of Campbell's warehouse, and later on a sum of £1 10s. was revealed. Both prisoners pleaded guilty and Mr Ambrose Jones, addressing the Court on behalf of Eatock, said he had borne a very good character, and was the son of a very respectable man.

Marriott had been the tempter in the case which, counsel thought, was one where the provisions of the First Offender's Act might be applied.

Evidence of the character was given for Eatock, who was then bound over to come up for judgement if called upon.

His Lordship warning him that he must be careful in his conduct. Marriott was sent to gaol for three months in the second division. His Lordship commented upon the creditable preparation of reports presented by police in the case.

James Wood was always a great champion of the old adage 'A place for everything and everything in its place', probably as a result of more than twenty years of military-style duties. He always insisted on looking clean and tidy, with his uniform pressed each day and buttons and boots shining in regulation order. He was also keen to ensure that his men followed suit and that they also had a good grasp of weights and measures and trading standards law.

When he was first appointed Manchester's Explosives Officer in the early 1900s, he accepted the challenge with relish. He put his army experience to good use and was used to dealing with high explosives and gunpowder storage.

In his role as a law enforcer under the Explosives Act, he took action against unlawful traders and firework manufacturers. He helped to clamp down on unauthorised sales and hit traders who either had no licence to sell fireworks, or, were well over their agreed and permitted quota.

His Chief Constable insisted on prosecutions, although I gather in certain cases, he left this task to the discretion of the senior officer. Below are some examples taken from Wood's own collection of newspaper cuttings which show what the traders could expect if they got on the wrong side of the law, together with copies of letters and relevant correspondence from regulating committees and the government.

Once again, it provides an interesting insight into the thoughts of senior officials at this period in time.

COPY OF LETTERS FROM TOWN CLERK.
APPOINTMENT AS INSPECTOR.
Meeting of the Watch Committee of the Council held on 8th January 1903.
Appointment of Inspector under the Explosives Act 1875.
Resolved: - that Sergeant James Wood be appointed as Inspector of the Local Authority of the City of Manchester under and for the purposes of the Explosives Act 1875 (a true extract).

CITY NEWS. October 18th, 1903.

FIREWORK SELLERS FINED.

Firework Sellers Fined – At the City Police Court on Wednesday, Michael Riley, trading as Riley & Sons, Lever Street, Piccadilly, was fined half a guinea and costs for permitting fireworks to be conveyed in an open cart without sufficient covering, and Henry Mann, the driver was fined one shilling and costs.

For improperly packing three parcels of fireworks, Riley was also mulcted [fined] in the sum of three shillings and costs. The Midland Railway Company was fined ten shillings and costs for insufficiently covering fireworks in a conveyance, and the driver, George Prescott, five shillings and costs.

For other offences under the Explosives Act, 1875, chiefly for exposing fireworks in shop windows, the following persons were fined: Elizabeth Howard, Lower Moss Lane, Hulme; Elizabeth Coleman, Hamilton Street, Rochdale Road; each one shilling and costs.

Katherine Walsh, Burton Street, Rochdale Road, half a crown and costs; Emily Edwards, Coupland Street, eight shillings and costs; Isaac Bradshaw, Mill Street, Bradford, five shillings and costs.

Inspector Wood prosecuted, the offences being proved by police constables Jones, Fisher, Scott and Brindley.

CITY NEWS, October 17th, 1903.

SHOPKEEPERS & THE SALE OF FIREWORKS

Nellie Kenworthy, Stockport Road, Longsight, was fined twenty-one shillings and costs for storing fireworks in unregistered premises. Ephraim Dickenson, Shakespeare Street. Chorlton on Medlock and Charles Wielding, City Road, Hulme, were each mulcted in the sums for storing more than fifty pounds weight of fireworks.

The prosecutions were at the instance of Inspector Wood, the offences being proved by officers Jones, Fisher, Scott and Brindley, who had previously warned the defendants.

Evening Chronicle, October 19th 1903.

ALARMING THE LADIES

For discharging fireworks on the highway, John Hawe (14), Weaste and Thomas Scalsh (15), Patricroft, were fined 5s each at Eccles today and warned that they were liable to a penalty of £5.

The thriving city – junction of Market Street and Exchange Street, 1902.
[Manchester City Library]

On Sunday night, as people were leaving church, the two boys were using 'throw downs,' among the crowd and alarming the ladies. They claimed that there was no fire and the crackers were harmless.

Evening News, October 29th 1903.
FIREWORKS DEALERS FINED
At the City Police Courts this morning, the following shopkeepers were fined for offences under the Explosives Act, 1875: - William Tierman, German Street, Oldham Road, for keeping four and half pounds of fireworks on unregistered premises, 5s and costs.

Betsy Greatorex, Upper Medlock Street, keeping seven pounds of fireworks on unregistered premises, 20s and costs. Ann Bailey, Moston Lane, exposing thirty-three and a half pounds of fireworks in a shop, 5s and costs. John Williamson, Moston Lane, keeping one hundred and eighty pounds of fireworks, or one hundred and thirty pounds in excess of the quantity allowed, 20s and costs.

Christopher Croasdale Hyde Road, Ardwick, for keeping one hundred and forty-seven pounds, in excess, 20s and costs. George Myers, Thomas Street, keeping one hundred and twenty-one pounds in excess, 20s and costs, and for not keeping in accordance with the Act, 20s and costs.

Henry Perks, Edge Street, keeping twenty-seven pounds in excess, 20s and costs, and not keeping in accordance with the Act, 20s and costs. Henry Clinton, Every Street, Ancoats, keeping three and a quarter pounds of gunpowder on unregistered premises, 5s and costs. Henry Lanson, Ashton Old Road, keeping two hundred and two pounds in excess, 20s and costs.

The prosecutions were taken at the instance of Inspector Wood, and the offences were proved by police constables J. Scott, Fisher, Jones and Brindley.

Evening News. November 12th 1903.
THE STORAGE OF EXPLOSIVES.
Prosecutions in Manchester.
The following persons were summoned at the City Police Courts today, under the Explosives Act, 1875, and were dealt with as follows: -

Hannah Whitehead, 82 Medlock Street, Hulme, keeping sixteen pounds of gunpowder in unregistered premises, 1s and costs. Robert Henry Hunter, 35 Rochdale Road, keeping sixty-seven pounds of fireworks in his shop, being nineteen pounds in excess, 10s 6d with costs, and for exposing eight and a half pounds on shelves, 2s 6d with costs. Sarah Woodhall, 26 Queen Street, Ardwick, keeping eight and a half pounds of fireworks, not being registered, 5s and costs.

Samuel Holmes, 109 Ashton Old Road, keeping four and a half pounds of fireworks, not registered, 5s and costs. Thomas Gee, 259 Stockport Road, keeping eighty-five pounds of fireworks, or thirty-five pounds in excess, 10s and 6d and costs, and for exposing thirty-one pounds in a glass case, 1s and costs.

Edward Tipping, 7 Ladybarn Lane, keeping sixty pounds in unregistered premises, 21s and costs. Ernest Holland, 2 Burgon's Buildings, Fallowfield, keeping eighty-six pounds of fireworks, unregistered, 5s and costs. George Brown, 3 Burgon's Buildings, Fallowfield, storing eighty-six pounds of fireworks, or thirty-six pounds in excess, 5s and costs, and for being the owner of eighty-seven pounds of fireworks and allowing the same to be stored in unregistered premises, 5s and costs.

A horse-drawn Manchester Police vehicle with support crew. [Greater Manchester Police Museum]

Inspector Wood prosecuted and the offences were proved by officer Richard Dorricott, Scott, Fisher, Jones and Brindley.

Evening News. November 25th 1903.
OFFENCES AGAINST THE EXPLOSIVES ACT.
At the Manchester City Police Court this morning, James Pain and Sons, firework manufacturers, were fined £5 and costs for having fireworks packed in cardboard boxes instead of cases of wood or other solid material.

They were also fined a similar sum for not labelling packages with the word 'Explosive.' The main parcel company were fined 21s. and costs for having exposed iron on a lorry whist conveying explosives. Mr Bell of the Town Hall Clerk's department prosecuted, and Inspector Wood and other officers proved the cases.

Evening News. December 17th 1903.
AN ERRONEOUS IMPRESSION.
James William Parrish, Dry Salter, of Caernarfon Street, Cheetham Hill Road, was fined 10s. 6d. and costs at Manchester City Police Court this morning for storing thirteen pounds weight of throw-down crackers without being registered.

This will serve to show that the impression that these crackers are not explosives is erroneous. Sergeant Wood and police constable Dorricott proved the case.

5. Social Reforms

One of James Wood's most noteworthy achievements was in working with a team of fellow Manchester police officers to provide destitute children with sufficient food, warm clothing and shelter throughout many desperate winters.

He also encouraged constables to report any incidences of potential neglect with children left wandering the streets in need of assistance. These cases were dealt with sympathetically and every effort was made to locate and provide help and support to the parents and families, and wherever possible to secure regular employment for the head of the household.

James Wood was also appointed a member of a special Council Committee and had peculiar responsibilities to oversee and execute regulations relating to Street Trading, the Licensing of Theatrical Children and the Explosives Act of 1875.

Manchester Chronicle, October 17th 1903.
MANCHESTER'S DESTITUTE CHILDREN.
Clothed by the Aid of the Police.
The policeman, whose duty it is to patrol the streets of Manchester, probably sees more of the squalor and poverty inevitably associated with large cities of population than anyone else, not even excepting the self-sacrificing ladies and gentlemen who visit the poor in the interests of one or other of the many organisations designed to help the poor and unfortunate.

And so the Police-Aided Association for Clothing the Destitute of Manchester – now in its second year – is doing splendid work among the wretched little children who run about the streets in tattered garments, or are confined to the house because they have not sufficient clothing even for decency's sake.

The system under which the Association carries on its essential work is briefly this:

The office of Chief Constable Peacock. [Greater Manchester Police Museum]

The police undertake to ascertain the homes of any insufficiently clothed children they may see in the streets, to find out the causes, which have led to their apparently destitute condition; and then to fill up and return to the Association, forms giving all the particulars thus ascertained.

These forms are then handed over to visitors appointed by the Association, who have voluntarily undertaken the work of making further inquiries. In the first year of the Association's beneficent operations, 335 children were clothed. This year, the number has reached 567 boys and girls.

This morning what may be described as the winter session was entered upon at the Albert Street police station, where clothing was distributed to 51 children. In this work, the police play no part. It is expediously but very kindly performed by members of the committee, of whom Mr James Scotson and Mrs Manton, assisted by Mr W. R. C. Clarke, the secretary, were present this morning.

The children, accompanied by their mothers or fathers in nearly every case, are received in the parade room, and then, one by one, in their 'shreds and patches,' are taken to an upper room, where in the case of a boy, he is given first a new shirt, and than a suit of warm navy-blue serge clothes.

As may be imaged, the transformation is in nearly every case, a startling one, and it is to be made complete when the well-worn shoes have been cast off and warm stockings and clogs substituted.

Never was the old saying: 'Fine feathers make fine birds' better illustrated. Boys who had entered the building looking half-starved and pitiably miserable off-springs of a poverty-stricken home – and natural inheritors of all that such conditions involve – looked positively well on the way to become sturdy little fellows with the makings of men and respectable citizens in them.

For that reason, the mothers looked thankful, and not infrequently, the busy workers of such a great good, shed tears of joy as the little ones pattered off in their warm clogs and clothing.

Further examples of the success in monitoring street trading and the difficult life of children on Manchester's streets are further explained and highlighted in the *Manchester Courier* of Tuesday, 9 May 1905; and by 'A Distressing Case' published in the *Manchester Evening News,* Saturday 9 December, 1905.

Police officers receiving instruction in shorthand. [Greater Manchester Police Museum]

December 10th 1903.

MANCHESTER WATCH COMMITTEE REPORT.

Re: Promotion of Street Trading Department Officers.

The Chief Constable begs to bring before the Committee the following facts and recommendations relative to the Officers of the Street Trading Dept.

The Street Trading Department was established nearly two years ago under the Manchester Corporation Act, 1901. Sergeant Wood was selected to take charge of the new department, and he was given the assistance of Constables Charles Dorricott and Richard Dorricott.

The officers entered thoroughly into the spirit of the Act and have by their exertions contributed in no small degree to the success that has attended the establishment and operation of the Department.

They have given entire satisfaction to the Chief Constable and the Committee, in their first annual report, issued last May, made the following comments respecting the Officers named, viz.,

'The members of the Sub-Committee desire to express their appreciation of the admirable work done by the Officers appointed to the specific duties of the Department by the Watch Committee and the Chief Constable.

'These Officers have exercised a friendly supervision over the juvenile traders of the City, and have encouraged them to improve their personal appearance. In several instances, they have been the means of obtaining permanent situations for boys previously engaged in street trading.

'They have also brought cases to light where parents have ill-treated their children, and where their earnings are squandered in vice and debauchery...and have taken steps which led to the punishment of the offending parents and the protection of their off-spring.'

The Chief Constable fully endorses this report. Sergeant Wood is also duly appointed (by the Watch Committee) Inspector under the Explosives Act for the City of Manchester. In the discharge of his duty, he is assisted by Constables Dorricott.'

The same energy has been shown in the administration of the Explosives Act as has been shown in dealing with Street Trading Regulations, and the Explosives Act are now better administered in Manchester than at any other period.

On Saturday last, Major Cooper-Keys, H.M. Inspector of Explosives, made a surprise visit to the City, and after examining the books, registers, etc, expressed his entire satisfaction with the same and intimated that he would have pleasure in presenting a favourable report.

The Chief Constable proposes to relegate the work in connection with the Registration of Domestic Servants (which comes into active operation on the 1st January next) to the Street Trading Department. It is advisable that an officer having such responsible duties should have a substantive rank.

Sergeant Wood has served in the Manchester City Police Force for over 13 years, has held the rank of Sergeant for nearly four years, is an officer of exemplary character, and during the whole of his service has never been late for duty, nor had any mark of any description recorded against his character.

PC Charles Dorricott has served 13 years and has only two minor offences recorded against him, the last being nearly 10 years ago. The Chief Constable therefore recommends that Sergeant James Wood be promoted to the rank of Inspector; that PC Charles Dorricott and PC Richard Dorricott, be each promoted to the rank of Sergeant.

Resolved: That the report now read, be approved, and the recommendations therein adopted, viz., that Sergeant James Wood be promoted to the rank of Inspector, and that PC Charles Dorricott and PC Richard Dorricott, be promoted to the rank of Sergeant.

The Manchester Courier, Tuesday May 9th 1905.
JUVENILE STREET TRADING.
Manchester byelaw at work.
Whatever may be the evils of street trading – and that they are considerable cannot be denied – they are being reduced to something like a minimum in Manchester. This much may not unreasonably be claimed as a result of the limitations now in force.

Three years' working of the byelaw adopted by the Manchester Corporation has produced striking results. The child of really tender years has been eliminated from the ranks of the street sellers, while the conditions imposed on those who remain have led to the practical disappearance of the old-time gamin.

The Manchester juvenile street-trader in the main is of a sturdy type, healthy and comparatively well clad, and except on occasions when the weather is unusually bad, rejoicing apparently in the free and unconfirmed nature of his calling.

Street traders in Rochdale Road, 1900. [Manchester City Library]

Scope of the Regulations

To recall briefly the purport of the bye-law of the Manchester Corporation, which came into operation on the 25th March, 1902, it may be stated that it provides, among other things: 'That no licence shall be granted to any child under twelve years of age. All children over that age, being boys or girls under sixteen, shall be entitled to be licensed, provided the Corporation are satisfied – (a), that they intend to trade in the streets of the city; (b), that they are not unfit to trade through being sickly, blind, deaf, dumb, deformed, or mentally deficient; (c), that they have the consent of their being licensed of the persons purporting to have the custody, charge or care of them, if such persons are fit persons, and have fit homes. Provided that in the case of girls under the age of fourteen, it shall be a condition of the licence that they shall not trade within an area of one mile from the Town Hall.'

Certain conditions have to be observed by the holder of a licence. These require that: 'No licensed child shall be in any street for the purpose of trading after eight o'clock at night between October 1st and the 31st March, or after nine o'clock at night between April 1st and September 30th.

'No licensed child shall trade in the streets unless decently clothed. No licensed child shall, whilst trading, be assisted by any unlicensed child. No licensed child shall trade at any time unless wearing his or her badge in the appointed way. No licensed child, unless exempt from school attendance, shall trade on the streets during such hours.'

Humane & helpful

So much for the restrictive side of the Corporation's endeavours. But the city authorities do not stop at a merely negative policy. Acts of Parliament and local byelaws depend for their success very largely on the spirit in which they are put into operation. One of the most gratifying features of the Manchester juvenile street-trading byelaw is the humane and helpful personal interest it has called forth in those who are concerned in the administration of the regulations.

The licensed sellers in the city – and one has reluctantly to point out that in this movement, Salford as yet, takes neither part nor lot – are the objects of an almost parental attention from the members of the Street Trading Committee of the Corporation, of which Councillor P Whyman is the chairman; the Street Trading Department of the City Police Force, over which Inspector Wood presides; and the police-aided Association for the Clothing of Destitute Children, of which Mr W. R. C. Clarke is the secretary.

The last named organisation came into being contemporaneously with the department, and is doing incalculable good in seeing that those holding licences are something like reasonably clad.

No deserving case reported to them by the police fails to receive assistance, and it will be readily understood that such cases are of constant occurrence.

The harvest of the street

The Association, in conjunction with the Street Trading Department, also exerts itself as far as possible to find regular employment for such of the juvenile traders as desire it. One of the great dangers of street trading is that those engaged in it may come to lose the taste for more staid and settled occupations.

It is a primary object of the Street Trading Department to try and counteract this tendency and to discourage a continuance in street trading beyond the age at which more settled work would be commenced. As showing the attention bestowed on this matter, it may be stated that regular employment has been found of the lads since October last.

But the emoluments of street trading are in some cases considerable, and to those who consider the present rather than the future, they offer some temptation to continue in the calling. We are credibly informed that some lads, while attending school full time, can earn as much as seven or

A police officer on duty in Market Street. [Greater Manchester Police Museum]

eight shillings a week from the sale of papers.

Regular vendors of newspapers on the streets, during the racing season, are said in not a few instances to clear from thirty to thirty-five shillings per week. Apparently, there is money to be made out of enterprising street hawking.

One veteran for many years, a familiar figure on Market Street, is credited with being the possessor of a bank balance running into some hundreds of pounds. But the prosperity of the few must not be taken as bearing any relation to the condition of the many.

Regular street hawkers for the most part fail to make their vocation yield anything more than a very precarious livelihood, sometimes, we fear, scarcely that. The general all-time average earnings of the juvenile section of street traders are estimated at from three to four shillings weekly.

Beneficial effects
The effect of the byelaw in thinning the ranks of the street hawkers has been enormous. In the days of unrestricted street-selling, it is estimated that something like five thousand children were so engaged in Manchester,

their ages ranging from so low as five years, and they were to be found on the streets at late hours of the night.

The average number of street traders licensed is now about eleven hundred. Nor can it be said that the reduction has entailed hardship on poor parents. Before licences came into operation, it was found that lads took to the selling of newspapers of their own accord, and without the knowledge of their parents, spending their earnings on sweets and cigarettes.

A vast number was also turned out on to the streets by callous parents, anxious only that their offspring should provide them with money for drink. Needless to say, anything of this character is practically impossible now.

Gambling among the hordes of street trading children, at one time said to be alarmingly prevalent, is now almost non-existent, while improved school attendance returns attest the beneficial effects the new regulations have had in checking a prolific source of leakage in the education arrangements of the city.

Evening News, Saturday, December 9th 1905.
A DISTRESSING CHORLTON CASE
Prompt relief work.
Particulars of a lamentable case of destitution in Chorlton-on-Medlock, have been supplied to us by Manchester police. The story is a distressing one, but it serves, at any rate, to show how promptly and effectively existing organisations are able to give relief when the necessity arises.

Sergeants Dorricott and Cox, whilst passing down London Road, met a poorly clad lad, who they thought was begging. They took him to his home in Tell Street, Chorlton-on-Medlock, where they found that the lad was the son of a commercial traveller named John Carroll, who has been out of employment for six months.

Mrs Carroll and six children were in a destitute condition. The ages of the children ranged from 18 months to 17-years, and the eldest lad had been unable to do any work for eleven weeks owing to an injury to his wrist.

The youngest child was suffering from measles. The only furniture in the house was a table, a chair and an old sofa; everything else had been pawned to buy food. When the officers visited the house there was not a scrap of food in the property.

The case was reported at the Town Hall to Inspector Wood, who communicated by telephone with the Rev William Johnson at the Central Hall. Within half an hour, one of the two sisters was at the house.

She obtained two shillings-worth of groceries for the family, left them tickets for more food for the weekend, and through the Lord Mayor's Charity, coke and coal were supplied.

Clothing for the children was sent by the police-aided Clothing association, and this morning, the father and his eldest son, went to the Central Hall, where temporary employment was found for them.

6. A Policeman's Lot

The Lost Dog that saved Manchester United
During the course of his service with the Manchester Police, James Wood came into regular contact with a number of notable people including Arthur Balfour, a local MP who became Prime Minister and later served as Foreign Secretary; Alfred Harmsworth, newspaper proprietor and founder of the *Daily Mail*; and Sir Nigel Gresley, railway locomotive engineer, designer of the engine *Malard* which broke (and still holds) the world speed record for a steam locomotive at 126 miles per hour. He was also directly, or indirectly involved in a number of significant events in the story of Manchester at the dawn of the twentieth century.

A strange feature of the story of Manchester United is that the club may never have come into existence, had it not been for the city's police – and a lost dog! The curious tale of the dog – excuse the pun – is still legendary in the region and dates back to 1902, just before the original Newton Heath LYR (Lancashire & Yorkshire Railway) Football Team changed their name to Manchester United.

Founded in 1878 by an enthusiastic bunch of young railway workers at the local carriage and wagon works, the club had made tremendous strides since first joining the Football Alliance in 1889/90, and then being elected to the Football League, Division One in 1892/3. This progress however, came at a cost, with a full-time club secretary, professional players' wages to consider and the increased expenses of playing matches up and down the country in a national league.

By early 1902, following some indifferent results on the pitch, Newton Heath LYC was in severe financial difficulties. Desperate for cash, they held a series of fundraising events, with one staged at the village hall and organised by Heath captain, Henry Stafford. The intention was to raise at least £100 to help stave off bankruptcy.

A detachment of mounted police. [Greater Manchester Police Museum]

Stafford, a popular character, attended with his St Bernard dog, Major. As a publicity stunt, he tied a collecting box around the dog's neck, as if highlighting a definite rescue plea. During the event though, the dog escaped from the packed hall and vanished. The matter was then reported to the local police and Major was later found, slightly confused and wandering the streets, by a pub landlord. The man was unsure what to do with the pet and, unaware as to whom it belonged, decided to take it back to his pub where he showed the dog to a local businessman, John Henry Davies, who at that time was the managing director of Manchester Breweries. The dog seemed to take a liking to the man, so Davies paid the landlord for it and went home.

Perhaps guilt eventually got the better of Davies, and he began to make inquiries about the dog's true owner, and via the police, found it really belonged to the Newton Heath skipper. He contacted the club and invited the player to come and collect 'Major' from his home, whereby Stafford explained the circumstances behind the dog's disappearance. The two men formed an immediate bond and Davies took an interest in the club and offered to help financially. Davies later met with a small consortium of friends and local businessmen, who agreed to pay off the debts, on condition they changed the name and put the new management under their control.

All this was quickly agreed but deciding on a new name for the club became a major problem in itself and various suggestions were made, including Manchester Celtic and Manchester Central – which some directors said, sounded more like a railway station. Eventually, chief scout Louis Rocco announced: 'Gentleman, we have a Manchester United'.

The name was accepted and adopted, and the rest, as they say, is history. The club then introduced a new playing strip, abandoning the existing colours of white shirts and blue shorts for a new bold kit of red shirts, white shorts and black socks. And it seems that shortly after this, the club also gained the nickname of the 'Reds.'

The club played in various colours during their short life. The first being green and yellow halved shirts, and later white shirts with a deep red V-shape. The old green and yellow kit was later used in more recent times during the 1990s as United's commemorative away strip. The loss of the name of their local Newton Heath Loco was a bitter blow to regulars, for the Heathens, as they were then commonly known, had

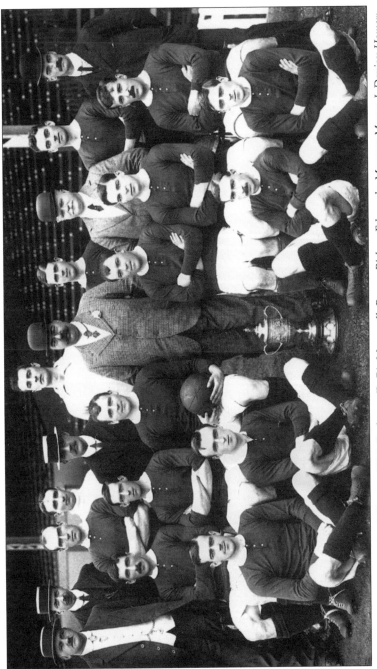

Manchester United F.A. Cup Winners, 1909. Back row (L–R): Mangnall; Bacon; Picken, Edmonds; Murray; Moger, J. Davies; Homer; Lawton, Bell Deakin. Middle row (L–R): Meredith; Duckworth; Roberts; Turnbull; West; Stacey. Front row (L–R): Whalley; Hofton; Halse; Wall.

fast gained a reputation for skill, flair and style, despite a rather heavy pitch.

Attendances were fairly healthy, with their first-ever home league match against Blackburn, attracting over 8,000 spectators. Many other games were equally well-attended but the new directors soon realised the bulk of support was not necessarily from locals, but from many others travelling in from far afield.

Much of the Heathens success – and problems – came after they had turned professional in 1885. The club had constantly attracted top players, including several Welsh internationals, because Newton Heath LYC, in addition to paying players' wages, could also provide additional regular employment on the railways.

In just twenty-four years, this small town amateur team of railway workers had achieved miracles and made unbelievable progress through the leagues. Their first ground was at North Road, close to an old clay pit, where players had to change in the local pub, the Three Crowns.

In later years and following re-organisation, they moved again, this time to a similarly muddy pitch across town at Bank Street, Clayton, where the players at least enjoyed the luxury of their own changing facilities – in a small wooden pavilion – yet had to endure the threat of heavy pollution from an adjacent chemical factory.

The ground was overshadowed and dominated by an enormous chimney, which often belched out black smoke across the pitch halfway through a match, and was surrounded by several daunting high walls.

Following the take-over and name change in 1902, the club's directors launched ambitious plans for future progress and decided to promote the club throughout the north-west. Six-years later, they made provision to build a brand new, state of the art, and purpose-built football stadium at Old Trafford.

James Wood, then a chief inspector in the Manchester force, was based at the police station at 627 Oldham Road, Newton Heath. He both lived and worked in the area, knew of the missing dog story, and spoke of mixed feelings for the proposed move. As a local resident and sporting man, he had witnessed a period of growth and the introduction of professional standards. He also knew the level of support and realised the potential impact such a move could have on the local community and economy. James Wood was a down to earth realist, and as a senior and very experienced police officer, responsible for many other major projects in the city, he was given the task of helping to evaluate this latest exciting development.

In 1909, Manchester United won the FA Cup, defeating Bristol City 1–0 at Crystal Palace, and by 1910 the club were in a very strong financial position to expand and were eager to move from their much-criticised Bank Street ground at Clayton to Old Trafford. Plans had been prepared a year or so before and were based on proposals from Archibald Leitch, a renowned architect and sports fan, who had already been involved with other similar schemes for Tottenham Hotspurs FC at White Hart Lane in London, and at both Ibrox Park and Hampden Park in Glasgow. Old Trafford cost a staggering £60,000 to build in 1910, but now boasted a fine seated and covered main stand, and three other large terraced areas, plus a superb grass pitch.

The fans and directors soon welcomed the move, and everyone understood the need to provide improved facilities, and to cater for the demands of supporters in this rapidly growing spectator sport. In 1911, their judgement was proved correct, when Old Trafford was selected by the Football League for an FA Cup Final replay between Bradford City and Newcastle United. Bradford eventually won the day 1–0, having previously drawn 0–0 at Crystal Palace. Just four years later, Manchester United staged the 1915 FA Cup Final at this stadium, when Sheffield United beat Chelsea 3–0.

What might have happened had it not been for that lost dog? And even more interesting, it is puzzling why there is little mention of this amazing story in the club's archives, and no certainly no memorial or dedication to the memory of this extraordinary dog.

A Royal Bodyguard, Foreign Agents and Agitators

One of the undoubted highlights of my great-grandfather's career was a temporary, although highly prestigious, appointment as Manchester's first official Royal bodyguard, during March 1902 when he played a vital role as an armed protection officer based within the Royal household for a special visit to the city by the Prince and Princess of Wales, Princess Louise, her husband the Duke of Argyll and many other distinguished VIP guests.

The true facts about James' role were mysteriously kept so secret that the press were only told about his unique involvement sometime after the visit – with many other details remaining under lock and key for several decades. At that time, James Wood was a detective sergeant and for this particular role, he worked in conjunction with a senior colleague, Detective Chief Inspector Corden, to help ensure the safety of the Royal party during an extensive three-day visit to the North West. The precise arrangements, which were all personally approved by the Prince, included a spectacular ceremonial procession, involving thirteen open-topped, horse-drawn carriages parading through the streets of Manchester to Owens College for the opening of the new Whitworth Hall, and later, a luncheon at the Town Hall, before finally travelling to Manchester Cathedral for the unveiling of a statue of Queen Victoria.

The initial part of James's duties included travelling as a security escort on the 'down' Royal train from London Euston to Huyton Station, near Liverpool, the day prior to the Manchester visit. Upon arrival at Huyton, he was instructed to accompany the party to Knowsley Hall, where he had to mingle unobtrusively with the many distinguished guests of the Earl and Countess of Derby. The following day, the Royals and all their guests travelled by train to Victoria Station, Manchester, to commence their official engagements. It was to be an historic day for the city, the very first Visit in State by the Prince and Princess of Wales and 'Heir Apparent'. City officials however, remained anxious about security and frequent threats to the Monarchy, but hoped this visit would lift the spirits of both the city and nation, following the end of Queen Victoria's incredible 64-year reign, just fourteen months earlier.

In addition, many believed it could also help introduce some of the next generation of Royals to an ever-curious public. In March 1902, the Prince's father, King Edward VII (fondly known as Bertie), was still five months away from his coronation at Westminster Abbey. Born in 1841, he had had to wait until his fifty-ninth year before finally succeeding to the throne. A most popular Royal, Edward, had married Princess Alexandra of Denmark in 1863, but unfortunately his own reign, in stark contrast to his mother, was short-lived.

This Manchester visit became an early and unexpected opportunity for Prince George of Wales to both meet and greet the people of the North West. George had been a professional naval officer until 1892 and was known as the 'Sailor Prince'. The second son of King Edward VII

The crowds wait for a royal visit near to Exchange Station, Manchester.
[Manchester City Library]

and Queen Alexandra, he became the 'Heir Apparent,' following the sudden death of his elder brother. George later met, and then in May 1893, married his late brother's fiancée, Mary, and they had four sons and a daughter.

This particular visit to Manchester rang alarm bells nationally, and came at a rather difficult and dangerous period for the Monarchy. Since Queen Victoria's extremely volatile Jubilee year of 1897, several threats had been made against members of the Royal Family, by what the government loosely termed 'Foreign Agents and Agitators.' This period also marked an uncertain and controversial time, when the country, if not the world, seemed to be in constant turmoil. There were a series of unprecedented attacks, bombings and threats of terrorism by Irish nationalist groups, and other militant organisations, as well as growing social unrest and mass demonstrations from unemployed workers. In addition, there was further trouble brewing within the turbulent Balkan States, and Britain was struggling to cope with an influx of immigrants from many so-called revolutionary countries. The

British Army was embroiled in several unpopular, expensive, and seemingly never-ending overseas conflicts. All in all, a scenario that was very similar to that of today.

Sergeant James Wood was thirty-four years of age, just three years younger than the Prince. He was well known for his prowess with weapons, explosives and self-defence. Archive notes confirm that he was also considered to be very tactful in delicate situations, which might therefore explain his selection for this extraordinary role. With the help of James's own cuttings book, personal notes, police records, photographs and newspaper archives, it has been possible to recreate a detailed account of this unusual Royal visit when, despite typical drizzly Manchester weather conditions, the city centre practically came to a standstill, and provided the Royal party with 'a tremendously colourful, and very splendid occasion.'

The event was witnessed by many hundreds of thousands of spectators, who eagerly packed the city streets, and every possible vantage point, just to catch a fleeting glimpse of the Royal visitors

Knowing the security headaches caused by this visit, and the potential threats from a varied assortment of agitators, it seems quite remarkable by today's standards, that much of the precise detail, including train times, order of carriage procession, and expected times of other arrivals and departures,were actually published the day before the trip [Tuesday, 11 March 1902] in many local and national newspapers.

The Royal party and their distinguished guests were to be transported in a procession of twelve official horse-drawn carriages, with another main carriage carrying the Prince and Princess of Wales, escorted by the Duke of Lancaster's Imperial Yeomanry. Although many workshops and warehouses remained open throughout the day of the visit, it was expected that many outdoor businesses would be suspended. Manchester was challenged by its own Lord Mayor to become a 'City of Festivities,' with tradesmen encouraged to wear 'festive garb' and to display colourful bunting as a sign of loyalty. Venetian masts were positioned along the route bearing banners and streamers boldly aloft, with beautiful floral decorations to be added at an early hour to make the scheme complete. Instructions were also given to display loyal mottoes and crests to prove the 'heartiness of the city,' and to welcome the Heir Apparent and his Princess. Many

Dense crowds of well-wishers gather at Manchester Town Hall.
[Manchester City Library]

business people with upper apartments, balconies or roof-top vantage points were generally persuaded to allow visitors to use their facilities for this rare occasion, and to witness the procession, with any monies received being donated to Saturday or Sunday Hospital funds.

At Owens College, preparations had been under way for some time with other numerous other universities and learned societies from across Europe well represented at their event. The college governors considered the opening of their new Whitworth Hall to be the leading part of the ceremony, and devised a programme to keep their visitors busily engaged for the best part of two hours.

At Manchester Town Hall, where James and his city detective colleagues were now housed in the basement, the building was bathed in flowers and foliage. This venue was also to become the focal point of the visit, where some 320 invited guests later attended a special luncheon with the Lord Mayor and their Royal party. And to keep the packed and patient crowds both settled and entertained, the Manchester City Police Band were deployed to perform in nearby Albert Square, playing some fifteen varied musical selections.

One of the final segments of a busy day for the Royals was an invitation to attend the city Cathedral after lunch, to unveil a statue of the late Queen Victoria in the west porch. Once again, exact details were revealed beforehand, the Cathedral clergy welcoming the Prince and Princess of Wales, the Earl and Countess of Derby, the Duke and Duchess of Devonshire, the Earl and Countess Spencer, Lord James of Hereford and Miss James, together with the Lord and Lady Mayoress.

It was said that visitors would also be able to enjoy musical accompaniment from the Band of the Manchester Volunteer Battalion of the Royal Medical Staff Corps. There was an air of curiosity at the Cathedral prior to the unveiling of the statue which was said to be both the work of, and a gift from Princess Louise, the Duchess of Argyle. It remained completely covered and hidden from the press, workers and officials until the moment of unveiling.

The Manchester City Police and representatives of the Army spent months scrutinising nearly minute detail concerning this visit, and agreed that a reception committee of local civic dignitaries should be the first people to welcome the Royal guests to the city. The reception party therefore included the Mayor, Recorder, and Town Clerk, who would all leave the Town Hall by carriage at 10.15 to attend Victoria Station, where they would be met by three officers and a hundred non-commissioned officers, from the 1st Battalion, The Manchester Regiment, resplendent in their black uniforms. The Royal Train was scheduled to arrive at 10.50 am from Knowsley. It was preceded by a pilot train which ensured that the track was safe and, after the latter had passed all points and junctions were sealed. Upon arrival, the Mayor introduced his guests, including Chief Constable, Robert Peacock, to members of the Royal party. A procession of open-topped, horse-drawn carriages then made its way to Owens College, travelling through the city centre along Market Street, Downing Street, Ardwick Green, Brunswick Street, Upper Brook Street and Dover Street. Following the visit to Owens College, the party retired to the Town Hall for a formal address and a luncheon scheduled for 2.15 pm. Later, the Royal visitors attended the Cathedral Street for the unveiling ceremony via Cross Street, St Anne's Square and Victoria.

Attention to detail was considered vitally important, even down to the make-up and schedule of the Royal Train, and to spectacular displays at both Victoria Station and the adjoining Hunts Bank and several other important locations within the city centre, where buildings and immediate area were blanketed in elaborate decorations, said to have been a joint initiative by line operators at the London & North Western Railway Company, and the Lancashire & Yorkshire Railway Company, who were co-owners of Hunts Bank. Victoria Station even enjoyed a bright new coat of paint for the occasion, which the press duly noted, and also made reference to the railway platform, which had been hastily converted from stone to wood, and covered by a bright new canvas.

Police notes confirmed the presence of James on the Royal Train which was supplied by the London & North Western Railway Company and comprised an engine and tender, brake carriage, two saloons, a Royal saloon, and a brake composite carriage. The Earl and Countess of Derby were to travel in the family saloon with their other guests from Knowsley, together with Colonel Fred Harrison, the general manager of the railway company. They were to follow the saloon, which was reserved for the Prince and Princess of Wales. Colonel Harrison, like James Wood, had travelled down from London to Huyton the previous day, and had then travelled aboard the Royal Train from Huyton to Manchester.

The press acknowledged all the unusual and colourful displays to help disguise some rather grim railway buildings and also noted a number of unusual incidents from an enthusiastic but sometimes anxious crowd of bystanders. They reported:

The spectacle between Hunt's Bank and the Victoria Hotel was of a memorable character. The route between these two points was thickly lined and it was evident from the character of the crowd that thousands upon thousands had come into the city for the purpose of witnessing the Royal procession.

The time of waiting was passed pleasantly and there was an abundance of incidents. As the Cathedral was passed, one or two of the bells were rung, it being evident that the ringers had either been misinformed as to the time of arrival of the Royal train or that they were testing the bells. The assemblage of so many brilliant and striking uniforms made the scene one, which will live in the memory of those who witnessed it. The spectators assembled about Hunt's Bank whiled their time away by the singing of loyal and patriotic songs, the first favourite being God bless the Prince of Wales, with Rule Britannia ranking next in the order of popularity.

At length a sound of escaping steam intimated to those nearest the station that the Prince and Princess had arrived. About this time, someone apparently in the neighbourhood of Victoria Station, fired a gun or let off a fog signal as a sort of Royal salute. The explosion startled a flock of pigeons. Immediately afterwards, the procession made its appearance, and the singing of the spectators was then exchanged for cheers, which were taken up and along the entire length of the route.

An incident, which caused some uneasiness at the start from Hunt's Bank, was due to the acclamations of the populace. The team of four dappled greys, which was drawing the open carriage conveying the Lord Mayor, became restive, and the near hind wheeler began to plunge. The coachman kept the horse under restraint admirably but his example seemed likely to be imitated by the horses of the Yeomanry and the mounted Infantry. A horse ridden by a policeman also became restive and dashed down Hunt's Bank, the rider losing his helmet in his efforts to bring the animal to a standstill.

The *Evening News* stated:

About five minutes to eleven the train steamed into the station and the first to alight from the Royal saloon was the Earl of Derby, the picture of a smiling and genial host. The distinguished visitors quickly alighted, while the guard of honour stood at the salute. The Prince, who was looking much stronger, and much more robust than on his former visit to Manchester, was attired in the ordinary garb of an English gentlemen; a thick overcoat protecting him from the coldness of the morning.

Her Royal Highness was attired in a handsome dress of heliotrope, with sable collar and sable muff, and wore a hat with violets. The Earl of Derby at once presented the Lord Mayor and Lady Mayoress, with whom the Prince and Princess shook hands. A similar recognition was given to a host of other civic officials and dignitaries, which also included Manchester City Police, Chief Constable, Robert Peacock.

This ceremony over, the ladies and gentlemen who had accompanied the Royal party entered the carriages in waiting. The Princess, meanwhile, continued in conversation with the Lord Mayor, and the Prince inspecting the Guard of Honour.

When he had walked along the two files of men, he rejoined the Princess and they entered the open carriage in waiting, drawn by four splendid bays with two outriders in the handsome livery of the Earl of Derby. Before her Highness took her seat, an attendant handed her a sable cape lined with ermine, which she wore during the drive, then amid the loud cheers of those at the station, taken up with alacrity by those outside, the procession started on the two-mile route to Owens College. ...

Past the Cathedral and the Victoria Hotel and then around the corner into Market Street, the cheering was again and again renewed. The thoroughfare presented a wonderful sight. Behind the barricades, the spectators were five and six deep, all the windows were occupied, and even the roofs were taken advantage of as well. Passing the big hotels in Piccadilly, it was noticed that the servants had taken possession of the top windows, and some of the women were on the roofs in most dangerous positions. At the corner of the Queen's Hotel there were banks of people who cheered as the procession passed. The most striking incident en route was observed near the London Road Station, the scene being the site of the new fire chief fire station at the corner of Whitworth Street. Here, a stand had been erected for the accommodation of school children, something like fifty-feet high, and providing space for thousands. At the foot of the stands were bands, which played the National Anthem and *God Save the Prince of Wales*.

The whole visit went like clockwork and was deemed a great success, due in no small part to the efforts of the Manchester Police, a fact which was acknowledged in a national newspaper report published the following day.

VISIT OF THE PRINCE OF WALES: Compliment to the Chief Constable. The police arrangements appear to have given satisfaction to all concerned, and at the close of the day's work, Mr Robert Peacock, the Chief Constable, received at Victoria Station, Manchester, an expression of approval from their Royal Highnesses.

The Prince of Wales beckoned to the Chief Constable and personally expressed his appreciation of the manner in which the police had done their duty. The Princess of Wales acquiesced in the remarks of the Prince, and remained for a few moments in conversation with Mr Peacock. The fact probably passed unnoticed yesterday by the crowd, that two Manchester Detectives personally attended the Royal visitors. Unfortunately, it is necessary that members of the Royal house in England, as well as rulers of continental nations, shall be protected from the possibility of attack by some madman or other, and with this object, Detective Chief Inspector Corden and Detective Sergeant Wood were included for the time amongst the members of the Royal suite. In the procession, they travelled immediately behind the Royal carriage, and indeed, were never far from their Royal Highnesses during the whole period of their stay.

7. 1905–06

In early 1905, James Wood was under strict instructions from the Chief Constable Robert Peacock, to clamp down on a number of key issues affecting the Manchester City authorities. In particular, these included several alleged breaches of juvenile performances in theatres; numerous bogus registrations of servants; and the need to tackle an unusual and unexpected influx of unsavoury material – including objectionable postcards – that were rapidly flooding seaside and tourist areas in particular. He was also required to act quickly upon other serious reports of so-called 'scandalous' publications that were becoming readily available in the Manchester area.

The following stories and newspaper cuttings reflect a sample of some of the many cases and convictions in which he was involved during this period:

30 January 1905, Evening News
JUVENILE PERFORMANCES.
The result of a breach of the Act
A music hall turn or theatrical performance of any kind by juveniles is nowadays subject to certain conditions, which are imposed on the parents or guardians under the Employment of Children's Act in the interests of the young performers.

A breach of the Act leads to police court proceedings, and a case of this kind was considered today by the City Stipendiary.

The defendant was Lachie Thompson, whose two sons, one under fourteen, were billed last December at the Metropole Theatre, Ashton Old Road, to give a boxing and wrestling performance.

The charges against Thompson were (1) with conducing to the commission of an offence by allowing his son to be employed on the stage at 9.35pm on the 28th December without having obtained a licence, and (2) with falsely representing the boy to be over fourteen years of age, whereby

A police officer escorts children during a Manchester Sunday school procession.
[Greater Manchester Police Museum]

he obtained employment for him.

Evidence was given by Inspectors R. Dorricott, Wood and Ogdon, of the performance of 'Lachie Thompson's Topweights' having taken place.

The offence was practically admitted by the defendant, who, however, pointed out that the lads were strong and healthy and the training had done them much good physically.

The manager of the Metropole stated there was a growing dislike amongst the artistes to take out licences owing to the great disparity in the charges made in different towns, ranging from a shilling to seven and sixpence.

A fine of 10s. and costs in each of the two cases – amounting altogether to £2 7s. 6d. – was imposed.

30 January 1905, Evening News
A LICENCE FOR CHILD ACROBATS

An application for a licence for the public performance of *The Butterflies*, two child acrobats, at the Manchester Hippodrome this week, was made today at the City Police Court.

The children are too young to perform without a licence, and Inspector Wood, objected to this permission being given unless with the condition that a net be provided. The applicant consented to this condition and the licence was granted.

Monday, 17 April 1905, Evening News
A BOGUS REGISTRY OFFICE.
Fraud at Chorlton-cum-Hardy.
Mr Edgar Brierley, second stipendiary, was occupied for some time at the City Police Court, this afternoon, investigating a series of charges of obtaining money by false pretences against Lizzie Clarke, a married woman, at present living in Bury New Road, Bolton.

The allegations against the prisoner were that through the medium of servants' registry office, which she had conducted in Warwick Road, Chorlton-cum-Hardy, she had obtained various small sums from persons who required servants and from servants requiring situations.

In the cases under consideration, she had not carried out the undertakings in these respects, and evidence was given by the persons concerned as to the falsity of her representations to those from whom she had obtained money.

The offences were brought home to her as the result of investigations by Detective Inspector Wood and Detective Sergeant Dorricott.

Mr Brierley said there was no doubt that the prisoner had been carrying on a fraudulent registry office. In 1902, she was convicted of fraudulently obtaining alms from charitable people, but was allowed to go.

Inspector Wood said a number of complaints had been received by the police in regard to the prisoner's conduct. Mr Brierley said he could not look over the offence, and the prisoner would have to go to gaol for six weeks with hard labour.

26 April 1905, Evening News
GOSSIP FROM 'TRUTH
At Manchester the other day, a Mrs Clarke was sentenced to six weeks' imprisonment for obtaining money from various persons by false pretences in connection with a servants' registry office.

Mrs Clarke merited her punishment but she may well be puzzled to understand why she is sent to gaol when so many other swindlers in the same line remain at large.

Certainly if she had set up her fraudulent registry office in London, she might have carried it on for years without any such disagreeable sequel in a police court.

19 August 1905, Daily Dispatch
OBJECTIONABLE POSTCARDS
Blackpool & New Brighton compared with Manchester.
Blackpool is not the only seaside resort where visitors are offended by the sight of indecent postcards,' said Mr E Jones Davies, the district secretary of the National Vigilance Association, to a Daily Dispatch representative.

Mr Davies added that New Brighton was also afflicted with the product of prurient foreign minds. He was doing what he could to suppress the sale and exhibition of such postcards.

Two complaints lately received about the state of affairs in Blackpool were, together with copies of the 'Daily Dispatch' containing the letters of complaint from its readers, being forwarded to the chief of Blackpool police.

Mr Davies hoped this action would be sufficient to check the pernicious practice. The same means were adopted in Manchester some time ago with excellent results.

Thousands of cards had been destroyed by order of the police. One wholesaler dealer, after prosecution, had gone round to his customers warning them against selling or exposing any of the objectionable pictures.

Manchester is more free from this form of evil than it has been since the picture postcard vogue began; said Mr Davies. 'Indeed, it is impossible for us to lay hands on a single card that is bad enough to warrant prosecution with hope of conviction.

The dealers are very careful not to run risks nowadays and I know that many of them make a practice of submitting samples of new cards for approval before offering them to the public.'

Indecency was, of course, largely a matter of opinion, said Mr Davies, and he was careful not to take proceedings except on pictures that must appear to any sane person as improper.

The Blackpool cards, he added, were not only indelicate, many of them were disgusting.

2 September 1905, Manchester Guardian
BALZAC'S *DROLL STORIES*

The seizure by the Manchester police of certain cheap translations of Balzac's works on Friday was followed on Saturday by the confiscation of a large number of copies of a penny edition of the *Droll Stories*, together with the type from which they had been printed.

It is said to be impossible now to purchase a copy of the English translation of Balzac's *Droll Stories* in Manchester, except by ordering it through a bookseller.

Hitherto, it appears, Balzac's works have been sold in Manchester both in French and in English without hindrance. Probably no one would have interfered with their sale now had it not come to the knowledge of the authorities that thousands of a cheap reprint of the least desirable of Balzac's *Droll Stories* were being printed and offered for sale.

Many complaints were made of the circulation of this reprint. The Chief Constable thereupon directed Detective Inspector Wood to make inquiries, and the result was that 15,000 copies of the work were seized on Friday and Saturday — not merely the penny reprint but other editions, ranging in price from one penny to three shillings, and in a few instances, even more.

It seems that the seizure of the offending books was accomplished on Friday with dramatic suddenness. Inspector Wood arranged that officers entrusted with the business should appear simultaneously at the place suspected of having books on sale.

In three or four instances, the booksellers tried to warn their neighbours of the police descent, but when their messengers arrived on the scene they found the police already there. Divining the object of the messengers, the police told them they were too late.

The further seizure made by the police on Saturday, led to proceedings before the City justices at Minshull Street Court on Saturday. The defendant, Mr James Miller, of Palace Street, Market Street, was summoned to show cause why a large number of copies of a certain book found on his premises and intended for publication should not be destroyed.

Detective Thomson said that on Friday afternoon, in company with Detective Sergeant Bloomfield, he visited the defendant's printing establishment. The defendant, when informed of the purpose of the visit, at once said that he had in his possession, copies of Balzac's *Droll Stories*, which he had printed and was quite willing to give them up if they were held to be indecent.

He led them to a room in the building and handed over 9,000 copies of the *Droll Stories*, which were removed to the Town Hall. The type from which the books were printed was subsequently taken possession of.

Mr Adams, solicitor (who represented the defendant), said: 'We may take it that Mr Miller gave you every assistance?'

Detective Thomson: Every assistance. He told us that he was ignorant of the character of the book that he had not read it at all, and simply printed it to order.

A JUSTIFIABLE SEIZURE

Replying to Magistrates Clerk (Mr Heywood), Mr Adams said that he did not contest the matter. Mr Miller was merely the printer of this work, which had been sold in many large establishments all over the country, just as he had printed other and perfectly innocent publications relating to wrestling, boxing and other games.

This one, he (Mr Adams) was bound to admit had been justifiably seized. The book was an abridgement of a well known classic – popular in the past, but not now admissible for public sale, particularly in penny editions and it might do a certain amount of harm.

With the consent not only of the printer but also of the publishers, he submitted to an order for the destruction of the entire stock. Only one thing he asked was that the defendant might have his type restored to him.

Mr Miller promised to exercise more care in the future and see that nothing was printed at his establishment that was of a questionable character. An order was made for the destruction of the books; the defendant's type to be returned to him.

Mr Adams wished, on the part of the publisher, to express regret that this had happened. He would take care that it did not happen again.

A DISCLAIMER

In Saturday's *Manchester Guardian*, it was stated that one of the shops visited by the police was in Cannon Street. Mr C. E. Smith, of 4 Cannon Street, writes to say that it is incorrect. He is the only bookseller in that street, and he has not sold any of the books to which exception is taken.

We understand that the shop in which some of the objectionable books were seized is in New Cannon Street.

A police recreation room with officers passing the time playing dominoes, billiards and weight-lifting. [Greater Manchester Police Museum]

THE 'CONTES DROLATIQUES

To the editor of the *Manchester Guardian*

Sir,

It was with much surprise I read the account in Saturday evening's paper of the raid by the Manchester police on the printing establishments. From the talk indulged in at court one is led to believe that Balzac's *Droll Stories* is a piece of very indecent literature, and that the book is not fit to be placed in the hands of any person.

This is far from true. *Droll Stories* is a volume written with a motive, and when well read and understood will prove a strong weapon in the hands of the moralist.

It is clean from cover to cover, and can only serve the turn of 'filth' in the hands of the filthy-minded. 'Virtus rectorem ducemque desiderat.' (Virtue requires the aid of a governor and director); vices are learned without a teacher.

Balzac in his works is a governor and director of virtues. Such is the opinion of yours & co. Marcus Duddleston, Pendlebury, September 2nd, 1905.

10 November 1905, Evening Chronicle
COUNCILLOR AND POSTCARDS

The 'housing' councillor for New Cross, Mr Marr, was asked last night, in the course of discussion on 'The Man in the Street,' what he thought should be done to deal with objectionable postcards displayed in shop windows.

Councillor Marr said his advice would be that the public should leave them severely alone. They got very little further forward in dealing with these things if they set up a policy merely of suppressing them.

Suppress them by all means if possible, but the policy of suppression was after all, a poor one, and he preferred to deal with the aspirations of 'the man in the street.'

If by their public policy they could elevate his tastes, then it would become extremely difficult to sell objectionable picture postcards with the ordinary business result.

Letter to the editor of the *Manchester Evening News*.

PICTURE POSTCARDS.

Sir,

Referring to your correspondent's remarks in yesterday's issue upon the display of indecent picture postcards in shops in Manchester, I should be obliged, with your permission, if I may inform the writer that if he will report anything of indecent character to Mr E Jones Davies, local secretary to the National Vigilance Association, 56 Peter Street, City, it will have his immediate attention.

The chairman of this Manchester branch was our noble citizen, the late Mr Herbert Philips, and this was one of the many institutions for moral purity, which had his support, and his lamentable death will be an untold loss.

I have reason to know that the authorities are very diligent in supporting anything of the above character coming to their notice.

29 November 1905, Evening News

PICTURE POSTCARD CRAZE.

Large numbers condemned by the Police.

The Manchester police have lately been turning their attention to the sale of picture postcards of an offensive kind, and Inspector Wood, and other officers have during the last ten days seized a large number of cards of various designs, together, in some instances, with the printing blocks.

Of the number of postcards seized, no fewer than 3,332 have been condemned as unfit for public sale. Over 1,000 of these were from one design, and they have been collected by the police from 46 shops in the city.

The procedure is to inquire of the shopkeepers whether they have any objection to giving the cards up, and in nearly every case their consent was obtained. Arthur Kay, a shopkeeper, of Ashton Old Road, was fined 5s. and costs at the City Police Court today for selling an offensive picture postcard to Detective Dorricott.

INDECENT POSTCARDS.

Over 3,000 seized in Manchester

The campaign in Manchester against indecent picture postcards, headed by Detective Inspector Wood is going apace.

During the past ten days, no fewer than 3,332 condemned postcards of various designs have been seized — and in some cases, the blocks also. Of one particular design, over 1,300 have been impounded from forty-six places.

It is only fair to the shopkeepers of Manchester to say that almost invariably when requested, they have raised no objections to giving up the offending postcards.

But Arthur Kay, of Ashton Old Road, point-blank refused to let Detective Sergeant Richard Dorricott have the specimen, which he had displayed, in the street showcase, and at the City Police Court today, he failed to see anything objectionable in it. The Stipendiary (Mr Brierley) thought otherwise, and fined him 5s. and costs.

In January 1906, eight candidates applied for the vacant post of Superintendent, viz:

Thomas Edwards, aged forty-eight, service 27 years and 11 months.
William Kearney, aged fifty-one, service 25 years and 4 months.

Frederick Knott, aged fifty, service 24 years and 11 months.
William Walker, aged forty-five, service 23 years and 6 months.
Walter Roome, aged forty-seven, service 23 years and 1 month.
William A. Wilkes, aged forty, service 18 yearsand 7 months.
Thomas Harper, aged thirty-eight, service 17 years and 10 months.
James Wood, aged thirty-eight, service 15 years and 2 months.

There were no adverse reports against any of the applicants and James Wood was the youngest candidate with the shortest length of service in the police. The position was awarded to William Walker, who had served for 5 years and 2 months in the rank of inspector. James Wood had only served 2 years and 2 months in the same position. It was to be another five years before he gained promotion to superintendent.

Just over three months later, Chief Inspector James Wood was commended for his activities in the position of Inspector of Explosives for Manchester. Before he had taken over, the various premises in the city designated as appropriate stores for explosives were deemed to be 'in a very indifferent condition'.   Major A. Cooper-Keys, HM Inspector of Explosives recorded:

Owing to his exertions however, I was able to report in the year 1903 that their condition was 'good' and in the year 1904 'very good' – the highest term of commendation we use. I may add that Inspector Wood gave me the impression that he is a man who would make every effort to perform in the most efficient manner any duties that he may undertake.

James Wood was officially appointed officer-in-charge of the Manchester City Police Courts in the spring of 1907, although the evidence would suggest that he had been overseeing the role since the spring of 1906. This appointment stemmed directly from his unprecedented success with other supervisory roles in key areas of the city's administration. This move led to a period of stability in his career which was welcomed after the wide-ranging responsibilities he had shouldered since joining the police service only a decade and a half previously.

James always had the welfare of his staff at heart and shortly after arriving at the City Courts, he was asked to evaluate the overall situation, and with the permission of his Chief Constable Mr R.

Peacock, prepared a detailed summary of his findings and proposals.

SPECIAL REPORT OF PARTICULAR OCCURRENCES
E. Division. Dated: 14th June 1907.
Inspector Wood respectfully begs to draw the attention of the Chief Constable to the business of the City Police Courts.

There are always three courts open daily in two of which, Inspectors are in charge, and the third, a Sergeant in charge. Very frequently it has happened that two or three extra courts have had to be opened in order to complete the day's work.

The staff of officers consists of two Inspectors and seven Sergeants; two Inspectors and three Sergeants only are available for Court duty and three Sergeants are permanently employed in the records, summons and property offices respectively. There is at present a vacancy for a Sergeant.

As it is necessary to have an officer in charge of each court, the staff of officers should be increased by the additional of one Sergeant, whose services could be utilised for Court duty and in taking charge of the vans used in collecting prisoners and their property each morning from several police stations and conveying prisoners and their property to gaol.

During the past twelve months there have been 15,863 summonses issued and 19,925 prisoners dealt with. As each prisoner is examined in order to obtain information for the guidance of the Justices, the records, His Majesty's Judges and the Governors of the Prisons, it will be seen that the work of the records office is very important and considerable and requires very careful and experienced officers to perform the work in connection therewith in order that an injustice shall not be done to a prisoner.

Other forces too, are continually asking for information respecting prisoners in their custody and of persons wanted by them.

The Inspector respectfully begs to suggest that the application for promotion to the rank of Sergeant made by E PC, Daniel Sweeney and E PC John McCreash be granted. Both Constables have been on the Court staff for several years and are well versed in Court routine and the work of the records office.

They are painstaking, obliging and courteous officers and in the event of their being promoted, PC Sweeney would be appointed to carry out the duties mentioned in the forepart of this report and PC Mc Creash would remain in the records office.

Mr Robson, Clerk to the Justices, had been spoken to by the Inspector and

James Wood.

he states that it is very essential to the dignity of a Court and to good order and discipline that an officer shall at all times be in charge of a Court and he therefore supports the Inspector in his application for an additional officer.

James remained in command of the City Courts until July 1911 when he was successful (in competition with twenty other candidates) in gaining promotion to the rank of superintendent and being given command of the city's B Division, based at Newton Heath. This promotion was confirmed by a Watch Committee report of 6 July 1911, making him, at forty-four years of age, the youngest superintendent on record. He was one of only a handful of promising officers who had worked their way through all departments of the force, from uniform to the detective office, and who was a proven master of clerical duties and administrative duties.

NEW POLICE SUPERINTENDENT
Appointment in Manchester.
The Manchester Watch Committee, at their meeting today appointed a superintendent to the vacancy caused by the retirement through ill health of Superintendent Corden.

There were 21 applications for the position and six of Inspectors of the City force were invited to meet the committee today. The successful applicant was Inspector Wood, who for the past five years has had charge of the City Police Courts.

He joined the force in 1890, and since has been in almost every department of the police service. He has passed through the uniform, detective and clerical branches, and has had charge of the street trading, servants' registry, explosive, and theatrical children's' licensing departments.

A popular officer, Superintendent Wood has made many friends whilst holding the responsible position at the City Courts and he has earned the respect of the Bench and his police colleagues, as well as of the other habitués of the courts.

8. Manchester's Air Race Drama

In April 1910, and following more than four years of prompting by the public and press, two intrepid flyers, Claude Grahame-White, an Englishman, and his French rival, Louis Paulhan, fuelled by the country's enthusiasm for aviation racing, agreed to take part in an exciting challenge, flying from London to Manchester in an attempt to win an incredible £10,000 prize offered by *Daily Mail* newspaper proprietor Lord Northcliffe. James Wood's daughter, Minnie, who was just sixteen years of age when the race took place, was taken out by a policeman during the early hours of the morning, to a rather wet and soggy field, to witness the arrival of a small biplane piloted by a young Frenchman. She recalled that, despite the early hour, there were some tens of thousands of people packed into, and all around, a small muddy field. She remembered a vast sea of faces and in later years thought the young pilot might have been Louis Bleriot, a recent champion of the Channel Crossing, and that the exact location might have been Platt Fields. Platt Fields was certainly the centre of many city attractions, including parades for Manchester Police but in this instance the landing site was a small grassy field close to Mr Bracegirdle's Farm at Burnage. And the pilot was not Bleriot, but a Louis Paulhan, another notable young Frenchman, who had just completed the 185-mile journey from London, via Lichfield, to win this extraordinary competition. The early morning start, vividly remembered by her, was due to Paulhan's sudden and unorthodox arrival at 5.30am. James Wood, who was then a Chief Inspector, had arranged a special treat for her and, perhaps due to his rank, had managed to secure her a 'bird's eye' view of the landing strip from the top of a police cart, where apparently she remained quite close to the plane for some time. Minnie was a very bright, attractive and popular young lady, who spoke a little French and may even have conversed with Paulhan. She certainly heard him speak briefly to the crowd, and to his assistants, amidst a great roar of appreciation from thousands of spectators. The plane was by then surrounded by a cordon of police officers to keep the public at bay. Within minutes of his arrival, Paulhan and his entourage were whisked away under police escort to the nearest railway station – and she recalled that everyone became soaked to the skin by some sort of bizarre 'tropical' downpour turning the field very quickly into a quagmire, and she recalled how engineers experienced great difficulty in removing the machine to a place of safety. In later years, the family believed this soaking led to James Wood developing pneumonia which resulted in a rapid deterioration in his health, a fate also suffered by some other VIP guests.

'Flying Machines', as these early aeroplanes were called, were noisy, smelly, dirty, unreliable and highly unpredictable. Such was the scepticism of the time that intrepid flyers such as Alberto Santos Dumont, Henri Farnam and even Wilbur Wright were struggling to reach any great height or distance with their own delicate contraptions. Indeed, in 1909, three years after the race launch, Wilbur Wright established a remarkable feat in flying for just over two hours in the United States, shortly before Frenchman Louis Bleriot, crossed the English Channel to claim a £1,000 prize. Bleriot went on to claim other cash prizes with a series of dare-devil performances both in France and abroad. Many machines were now being designed and developed by motor engineers based in and around Manchester. Charles Fletcher of Rusholme, who used his Stockport Road factory to produce cars and the first motor ambulance for Salford, began to take a keen interest in flying. He joined forces with Norman Crosland and William Arnold and encouraged a talented young apprentice John Alcock (later of Alcock & Brown fame) to share his enthusiasm for aviation matters. Fletcher built a single-seater monoplane, and utilised his own manufacturing facilities to develop new ideas based on French designs and powered by five-cylinder rotary engines. His trial flights though, were not without mishap and confirmed several obvious dangers. On 20 October 1909, he managed to fly about thirty yards in Heaton Park and made a few more attempts before finally coming to grief, colliding with the park's bandstand. Much of his progress was featured in the *Aero* magazine and highlighted the fact he made numerous 75 and 100 yard-long jumps, and confirmed that in January 1910, a strong wind had caused his plane to collide heavily with a clump of trees. A couple of months later, and just before the London to Manchester race, Fletcher

Claude Grahame-White.[The Times]

built another monoplane using parts from the wreck of his earlier plane, and exhibited his machine at White City. He continued with the testing and development of a new engine and biplane but after further mishaps, including an enforced landing in Salford's River Irwell. Fletcher was one of Manchester's first flyers and without doubt this early work encouraged a lot of other local men to follow in his example. The cost of production though often put flying out of the reach of many individuals, until certain parties began to pool their resources to help develop skills. Some enthusiasts opted to form a new aviators' club, which later became known as the Manchester Aero Club, and on 25 August 1909, prospective members attended a preliminary meeting at the Douglas Hotel on Corporation Street.

On 9 September, a further meeting was arranged at Manchester's Midland Hotel, which was attended by more than three hundred prospective members. It was here that new Club chairman William Bailey also discussed the possibility of an aerodrome at Trafford Park. The Club was supported by a host of experienced international flyers including Claude Grahame-White, Louis Bleriot, William Cody and A.V. Roe, who were each invited to become honorary members. A month before the Manchester air race in April 1910, Manchester's Lord Mayor opened a special Club exhibition of model planes at White City.

By the early years of the twentieth century, many national

newspapers were opening offices in Manchester. The London–Manchester race was seen as a perfect opportunity to promote the area and enhance the pioneering spirit of the North West and other towns such as Doncaster and Blackpool tried to muscle in on the aviation act with specific meetings and attractions, offering large cash prizes to prospective young flyers.

Details of this unique challenge were first published in 1906. At that time, very few flying machines were available and Lord Northcliffe (formerly Alfred Harmsworth, and a former associate of James), probably thought it was a safe bet, but welcomed the publicity, offering a staggering sum of money, £10,000 to the winner. This of course represented an absolute fortune at that time, with average wages for white-collar workers being around £100 per year, and general tradesmen only earning about half that amount. The Manchester Police had been on standby several times since 1906 in case any attempts were made to win the prize and were concerned about the problems such a large cash prize might cause. Just five days before Paulhan's flight, Grahame-White had made an unsuccessful solo attempt. The Manchester force, certain that Grahame-White would attempt to go again, and that his failure might well spark another pilot into action, awaited news from their London-based colleagues. What could the police expect? How many people were likely to attend the landing site? Would the actual site be where they envisaged? What emergency procedures were on hand? These were just some of the many imponderables worrying James Wood and his colleagues in the days immediately prior to successful completion of the race. The only definite fact known about these new machines – which did little to settle the nerves – was that they were highly unpredictable, with both the pilot and engines exposed to the elements. There were numerous basic problems to consider and James, in his capacity as the city's appointed explosives and regulations expert, constantly found his guidance sought and tested by a desperately worried Watch Committee. The air race posed many unique problems, not just by the thought of a potential 'flying bomb' crashing with gallons of petrol strapped to the fuselage in straddle tanks; but also the difficulties of trying to maintain law and order, and public safety with an excitable crowd confined into an unspecified area. James Wood, however, probably relished this exceptional challenge and was thrilled at the prospect of helping to supervise the safe landing and celebration of

Manchester's first ever flying-machine in some muddy field.

Although the event was something that had never been experienced in Manchester, city officials had been given a brief taste of the problems accompanying aeroplanes during a series of trials, a year or so before at Heaton Park, in north Manchester. Some trials by early pioneers had been staged in the Park, with others held on Salford Racecourse during 1909. Here, the actions of the participants were monitored by the police, and supervised; and yet despite the tranquil settings at these secluded sites, several trials still resulted in damage and severe personal injury. This latest escapade was a huge gamble, especially with thousands of spectators present, and coupled with the obvious dangers of transporting highly inflammable fuel by both air and rail. The whole episode presented a huge public risk.

The idea of a London–Manchester flight dated back to 17 November 1906, when newspaper chief, Lord Northcliffe, first announced details of his substantial cash prize to the first flyer to travel from a distance of five miles from the London headquarters of the *Daily Mail*, to alight within a similar distance from their Manchester office. The rules insisted that not more than two landings were permitted within a 24-hour journey and that the prize would be allocated for journeys in either direction. An additional incentive was offered by Adams Manufacturing Company, who proposed an extra sum of £2,000 to the successful winner, if they flew an all-British machine. An additional sponsor, *Autocar*, also suggested a prize of £400 to the maker of the winning engine – provided again, that it was of a British manufacture.

At the time of launching this challenge, the majority of people claimed it was 'mission impossible' and 'totally unobtainable.' It meant a flight of nearly two hundred miles cross-country between two great cities by inexperienced pilots in rather primitive, untried and unreliable machines. Nothing of note had been achieved at that particular time by early flyers and aviation development was still slow, risky and badly under-funded. To support this astonishing theory, and to highlight the magnitude of the undertaking, *Punch* magazine also offered the exact same prize money to the first man to swim the Atlantic – and also to the first person to reach Mars and back within a week!

The two main participants for the *Daily Mail* air race of 1910 were the Englishman, Claude Grahame-White, and his more experienced

French rival, Louis Paulhan. Grahame-White was called an 'exhibition flyer' and was said to be fascinated by aviation, always full of enthusiasm for the sport. The son of a wealthy businessman from a highly respected family, he studied engineering at university and successfully ran a motor dealership in London's plush Mayfair district. He became entranced by the prospect of flying and examined Bleriot's machine when it was displayed in Selfridge's London store. The following month, he travelled across to Rheims in France, telling all his friends and staff that he might return with a new aeroplane. He carefully examined all the machines before finally agreeing to purchase one of Bleriot's new aeroplanes, a Bleriot XII. He remained at the French factory for about two months during the construction and began testing the machine on a nearby runway, practising his techniques with a series of long hops before eventually taking off. Grahame-White immediately became obsessed with flying and in an attempt to continue with his new passion, started a flying-school in south-western France using several of Bleriot's latest machines.

By the spring of 1910, he had many regular pupils but said he intended to return at the first opportunity to compete in the *Daily Mail* Air Race, claiming the £10,000 prize money would provide the perfect opportunity to help launch a new flying-school in England. To achieve his ambition he purchased a new Farman biplane and arranged for it to be shipped across the Channel, so that he could begin training. Although most of his limited flying experience had been achieved in Bleriot machines, he believed the London–Manchester race was not possible in that type of plane with only two landings allowed. He believed his Henri Farman-designed machine offered greater speed and flexibility.

Farman, born in Paris to English parents, was a former cycling champion who had turned first to motor sport, and then to aviation. Although he won a major national aviation title in 1908, Farman's speciality was in flying at high altitude rather than at speed. He preferred designing and building the machines to actually flying them and concentrated his efforts in the manufacturing side of the business, but continued to help a number of pilots achieve their own personal ambitions.

Farman and his team of mechanics volunteered to help Grahame-White in his attempt to win the £10,000 prize, and even travelled to England with him on the ferry, complete with his new crated biplane.

Grahame-White was not, however, the first airman to state his intention to win this prestigious race. That particular honour was reserved for George Davidson, who had submitted a race entry in the autumn of 1909, but had to drop out of contention due to a lack of funds. Other potential cross-country flying champions included Edgar Wilson, Eugene Gratz, an ambitious young Frenchman named Dubonnet and Samuel Cody, who made the first powered flight in Britain. Cody went so far at to visit Lancashire and even selected a route in reverse from Manchester to London. Ingeniously, he also prepared for a series of smoke signals to be used en-route to assist with navigation.

At about the same time of Cody's visit, another challenger, the ruthlessly determined Frenchman, Louis Paulhan, suddenly appeared on the scene and carefully surveyed the route, taking a peculiar interest in the London & North Western Railway which ran directly from London Euston to Manchester. As Paulhan considered his options, Cody also re-assessed his journey plans and decided to take the more conventional route from London. And, similar to Davidson, he planned to challenge for the prize in the autumn of 1909. His attempt however, failed due to an engine seizure.

Claude Grahame-White studied all the efforts of these competitors and was both fascinated and delighted by the amount of publicity each attempt received. He too visited the Manchester area and inspected potential landing sites at Urmston and Chorlton-cum-Hardy. After much consideration, he finally selected another preferred site in a field adjacent to the railway station at Fog Lane, Burnage. A fact also duly noted by Louis Paulhan. Grahame-White even managed to persuade the L&NWR to assist his efforts by agreeing to colour certain sections of track with whitewash for several 100-yard stretches at major junctions. Due to the oncoming winter weather though, he postponed any attempt to win the prize until the following spring, believing no one else could better his preparations.

Greeted by his friend and associate, Henri Farman, a large supportive crowd and members of the Royal Aero Club, Claude Grahame-White first set off for Manchester on 23 April 1910. He took off in near darkness from Park Royal in favourable weather conditions, flying over a gasholder at Wormwood Scrubs, where an official waited to confirm the time and ensure his start was within five miles of the *Daily Mail's* London offices. He then carefully followed the train tracks towards Manchester. Crowds waited all along the route and cheered him on. They packed railway bridges and every possible vantage point. Many supporters also followed his journey in motorcars, but were unable to keep pace with his aeroplane. At Kilsby, near Northampton, one car, said to be hurrying along, and carrying some of his mechanics overturned, injuring several passengers.

Grahame-White was totally oblivious of the confusion and excitement on the ground. His own race programme seemed to be running to plan until he reached his pre-arranged landing site near Rugby where, despite a relatively smooth landing, he broke a strut on his undercarriage. He was glad to descend though as he was numb with cold and could be seen visibly shaking when he alighted at 7.20 am. During his journey he achieved a new British record, having covered a distance of seventy-five miles. He told friends he had been wretchedly cold all the way and said his eyes suffered and fingers suffered with the cold. He was taken by car to nearby Gellings Farm for a brief snack and hot drink whilst his assistants re-fuelled his machine. By 8.15 am he was off again, this time heading towards Crewe in Cheshire. By then, the wind had increased and his machine suffered severe buffeting and turbulence, forcing him to land again at Hademore near Lichfield.

At this point, Farman warned that conditions were too dangerous to continue. They waited all day for a break in the weather but at 7 pm, with the light fading, Grahame-White decided to abandon any further attempt that day. He considered that if he made a 3 am start early the next morning, he believed he could still win the prize – allowing just over two hours to reach Manchester within the 24-hour limit. At the appointed time however, the wind and storms continued, if not worsened, and the flyer told the waiting crowd that unfortunately, he would have to abandon his quest. He planned to fly on to Manchester to continue the attempt in reverse but his assistants failed to secure his plane to the ground with stakes and ropes, and it was later overturned and damaged by several strong gusts. His plane suffered a badly torn canvas with several broken struts. Bitterly disappointed, he immediately decided to return to London for repairs and said he hoped to make another attempt when the weather improved a couple of days later.

Meanwhile, Grahame-White's main continental rival, Louis Paulhan, who was in Cologne, watching German military aviation trials at the time of the failed attempt, celebrated the news. He made immediate plans to travel to Britain and notified the race organisers of his intention to compete for the prize. Paulhan hoped to take-off before the British flyer repaired his own machine. He knew time was against him and travelled directly to London.

In comparison to Grahame-White, Paulhan was a very experienced flyer who had won many cash prizes at several influential meetings. Like Henri Farman, he was also a high-flyer, preferring to travel at high altitude and enjoyed endurance events. This competition seemed ideal for a man of his capabilities and later that year he won a cash prize of £5,000 for the greatest number of competitive flights. Paulhan was also interested in training future pilots and in designing new aircraft including tri-planes for the French military. He also intended helping to develop a revolutionary new flying-boat or sea-plane in conjunction with Glen Curtiss, a fellow aviator, and former colleague of Grahame-White's.

Paulhan's racing plane was another Henri Farman designed biplane, but was totally different in style to that of his English rival. Paulhan's plane had two rear rudders in a box shape within the tail-plane. Grahame-White had only one central rudder and it was built with slightly lower wings for increased speed and mobility. The Englishman knew of Paulhan's expected challenge and worked solidly to repair his machine but remained hampered by strong winds. Paulhan too was having serious problems: his crated aeroplane which had followed him by boat to Folkestone, was too wide for the railway tunnels en route to London.

Despite a close association with both flyers, Henri Farman and his team of mechanics spent all Wednesday morning (27 April) preparing Grahame-White's aeroplane. When the work was completed, the pilot still considered it was too windy to leave and decided to retire and make an early start the following day. Paulhan however, quickly assembled his machine that same afternoon and, without any adequate testing, decided to make an immediate attempt, lifting off from near Hendon at 5.31 pm, in order to gain a slight advantage over the Englishman. This was a brilliant tactical move on his part, and obviously took his opponent completely by surprise. Grahame-White had to be awoken from his bed just before 6 pm to be told the news. Without hesitation, he ordered his machine to be withdrawn from the hangar and made ready, while he dressed.

Grahame-White's friends claimed he remained 'perfectly cool' and

Claude Grahame-White's aeroplane is pictured just prior to take-off in London, en-route to Manchester. [The Times]

yet 'frustrated and vexed' by Paulhan's pre-emptive manoeuvre. He was soon ready for take-off and departed, without having had any time to eat or drink, within half an hour of being woken, but was still nearly an hour behind his rival. Paulhan continued flying at a high altitude for 117 miles until he descended near Lichfield due to the failing light. Grahame-White though flew at low altitude and paid the price, constantly struggling against the buffeting wind and rain before descending at Roade, near Northampton, some sixty-one miles from London. This head-to-head challenge caught the imagination of the nation and every radio broadcast, newspaper and railway station trumpeted the latest news of this exceptional adventure.

The impending arrival in Manchester of one of the airmen was certainly a momentous event. Who was actually in charge on the ground still remains a mystery? Certainly the Chief Constable, Robert Peacock, would have had overall responsibility, and an Inspector Dickenson is mentioned in news reports as being in charge at the landing site. We also know that a large contingent of police officers was delegated for the purposes of public order and protection. James Wood certainly played an important role and was given some sort of additional advisory role prior to, and during, the event, both in his capacity as an experienced senior police officer, and as an explosives expert.

Since Grahame-White's initial attempt a few days earlier, many officers from the Manchester force had remained on standby for what eventually proved to be a momentous occasion.

On 29 April 1910, *The Times* reported:

The news that neither aviator could finish the journey on Wednesday night did not satisfy the large crowd that had assembled at Bracegirdle's Farm, New Burnage. They were not sure that a surprise was not in store for them. Some stayed at a neighbouring inn and slept on chairs, for it was realized that Mr Grahame-White must make a very early start if he was to make up lost time. At four o'clock there may have been a hundred persons present, and among these were several ladies. Some had come on foot and some on bicycles. At half-past four there were less than a thousand, but at five o'clock, there were three or four thousand people. Conflicting messages arrived, one to the effect that Mr Grahame-White had started at three o'clock, another saying that both competitors were flying, and that one was only 25 miles behind the other. At 5.15am, the official time-taker of the Royal Aero Club walked out to the centre of the field in which a white sheet lay on the ground. The sheet however, was not unrolled, for it was known that both aviators would recognise the field, and in an emergency, signals could be made.

At 5.25am, a report arrived by telephone at the signal box at the station that a flying machine was approaching, and that it had been seen from a point about five miles to the south. Not until that moment had the crowd fully realised the marvellous nature of the feat, of which they were now to see the completion but that pregnant message stopped the babel of voices, and the great crowd stood silently expectant.

Along the road to the south of the field the houses were fronted by a double row of motorcars. Thick lines of people marked the public paths at the sides and through the field, the platform of the high-level station to the east was thronged. Every eye was directed towards the skyline of the houses and the trees in the south. The western horizon was crimson with the light of a threatening sunrise' overhead the sky was dull grey, and a light cold drizzle was driving along on a south westerly wind, which at times blew at 15mph. Suddenly there was a scattered volley of exclamations: 'Here he is! Paulhan is coming!'

Over the tops of the trees he appeared, small and faint at first, but rapidly increasing in size, the now familiar outline of an aeroplane. From the crowd there arose cheer after cheer. No one cared then whether the aviator was Frenchman or Englishman. It was enough that he was a hero of the air. The manner of his coming too, was prophetic of so much yet to be achieved, that international and sporting rivalries seemed to be forgotten for the moment. The mixed crowd of working people, trades

Two very different types of 'mounted' police officers.
[Greater Manchester Police Museum]

people and country gentlemen appeared to have been filled with a deep consciousness of the significance of the event.

No such scene had ever before been witnessed. A sense of awe prevailed for an instant, and then the crowd threw off all restraint and streamed across the field in one wild rush. The volume of cheering grew and grew until it became deafening. Men and women shouted incoherently. M. Paulhan, for it was soon known that it was him by the pair of vertical planes visible in the tail of his machine – flew at a height of about 1,000ft. Then sweeping in a vast circle eastwards, he passed over the railway and descended lower and lower until some thought he would land on the other side. He turned however, westwards, and surmounted the raised railway line and the telegraph wires, watched anxiously by thousands of eyes, he completed the half-round and headed towards the south, descending all the time, until at last he touched the earth at 5.30am, welcomed by the cheering of thousands.

He had been half frozen with the cold, but he was warm enough in a few seconds. The one overmastering desire of every man and every woman in the crowd was to grasp his hands. He smiled but could not utter a word. Then, as police forced their way through to his rescue, he realised the generosity of the people who gave their countryman's rival such unstilted honour. Rising in his seat, he raised one hand, laughed joyously, let his eyes dwell fondly on the sea of faces, and allowed himself to be hauled down. Guarded by two policemen, and surrounded by a ring of protectors, he hurried towards the station accompanied by a dense mass of cheering people, who almost fell over each other in the rush. It was hard work for the police but they got their charge safely through the wicket and up to the steps of the platform where, a few minutes earlier, the special train had arrived. The crowd all this time had continued to cheer and call for 'Paulhan' until the train was out of sight.

The *Manchester Evening News* stated:

There was a strong easterly wind blowing over Burnage and district at daybreak and it seemed doubtful to the large crowds awaiting the arrival of the flying-man in Mr Bracegirdle's field, off Fog Lane, whether it would be possible for either of them to complete the long journey, and so win the £10,000 prize. However, by five o'clock, word was passed round that Paulhan was well on his way and might be expected at any minute. Excitement naturally ran high, and there was tremendous enthusiasm, when a few minutes before half-past five, the daring Frenchman was seen steering his graceful bi-plane high over Fog Lane.

Instead of dropping straight into the field, which skirts the railway within a few yards of the new Burnage station on the London & North Western Railway Company's Styal line. Paulhan flew on for another quarter of a mile or so in the direction of Ladybarn, and then, making a wide circle, came down exactly at half-past five with a gentle swoop right on the appointed spot, without the slightest mishap. The motor was stopped the second the machine reached earth and Paulhan was enthusiastically cheered as he steeped from his seat to the ground. Disappointed as the immense crowd naturally knew that Grahame-White had not succeeded in winning the great prize, it was too sportsmanlike to allow this fact to distract from the heartiness of the welcome accorded to the victor, and Paulhan was enthusiastically cheered as he stepped from his seat to the ground.

There were loud cries for a speech but Paulhan simply remarked that it had been very cold, could not be prevailed upon to accede to the demand, and accompanied by those of his friends who by this time had gathered round, and followed by the cheering crowd, he made his way to Burnage station, where a special train was now in waiting to convey him to Manchester. On the station platform Paulhan was the subject of a friendly mobbing, everyone being anxious to shake hands with the man who had accomplished so great a task, and there were again calls for a speech.

Still the Frenchman was not to be drawn, though he repeatedly acknowledged with bows and smiles and ejaculations of the word '*Merci*' the compliments showered upon him. The meeting of Paulhan and his wife at the station was a very touching spectacle. Madame Paulhan threw her arms around her husband's neck and kissed him repeatedly. The aviator and his party, including M. Farman, then boarded the train and within 30 minutes from the time the aeroplane landed, Paulhan, his wife and friends were on their way to London Road station.

The *Manchester Evening News* went on to describe the problems encountered on the field whilst dismantling the aeroplane.

A rainstorm, almost tropical in severity, passed over Burnage and considerably impeded the work of dismantling the aeroplane. Indeed, a sudden gust of wind at a critical moment almost overturned the undercarriage, which had been detached from the rest of the machine. One of the straps was broken, but fortunately the damage was not serious, and the work proceeded without further incident.

The thousands of people however, who had gathered round by this time were drenched to the skin, and the growing crop of clover upon which M. Paulhan had descended was in a sorry plight. For many yards circumference round the machine, it was trodden into an undistinguishable mess and the damage thus done must be very great. In spite of the weather the crowd waited hoping to be present at Mr White's descent should it be at the spot. Rain continued to fall heavily and as information on the whereabouts of Mr Grahame-White being unobtainable, the crowd at last disappeared and a mere handful of spectators remained on the ground.

It is right to say that the behaviour of the public throughout had been admirable, and the police who were in attendance under the direction of Inspector Dickenson had very little work to do in the maintenance of order, or preventing damage to the aeroplane.

Grahame-White, meanwhile, had continued with his attempt to complete the course. After leaving Polesworth, however, he made very little progress and took half an hour to cover 8 miles. He eventually landed at Whittington near to where he had landed on 23rd April.

9. The End of a Glittering Career

This was a very difficult section to research and publicise for obvious personal and family reasons, and as it provided a rather dramatic and totally unexpected chapter in James Wood's life and career. As a highly respected senior police officer, he was very experienced, and yet, and probably for that very reason, became an easy target for potentially vindictive and disgruntled officers. He was not, I might add, the only target for malicious gossip, innuendo and abuse as many other senior officers suffered a similar fate, all of whom had to be fully investigated by the appropriate authorities.

From 1913 onwards, however, James began to suffer from bouts of ill health. Family members were convinced these problems took hold shortly after James received a thorough soaking during the Manchester–London Air Race in 1910. It is certainly known that he later caught pneumonia at least once, and was consequently left with a weak heart. The job, however, remained extremely demanding and he hardly took any time off. He was often on call seven days a week, twenty-four hours a day, and like many other senior officers, he lived above his police station. He was one of only a handful of experienced front line superintendents, and since becoming the youngest officer to achieve that rank in 1911, was seemingly determined to prove his worth.

Bribery, fraud and corruption were rampant at this time, and it had been James's job to investigate a great number of allegations against fellow serving police officers, and subsequently, it became a most unpopular task. He acted under direct instruction from the Chief Constable, Robert Peacock, who was determined to rule with an iron rod. James was called upon to investigate claims of bribery and dishonesty against two constables – and yet just a few months after completing his report (with the aid of two sergeants), he found himself being accused of wrong-doings by one particular aggrieved individual. This officer made several unfounded accusations against James and his two sergeants, and subsequently claimed damages for unlawful imprisonment and trespass. All charges were of course denied and

James Wood (front left) taking part in an inspection of the Manchester police.
[Greater Manchester Police Museum]

defended; but the accusing officer's complaint had to be duly investigated, with a report passed to the Chief Constable for consideration.

A lowly constable's life during that period was not considered to be particularly rosy. The job offered poor pay and relatively poor working conditions, with many restrictions placed upon their personal lives. Many officers left the service after just a short trial, whilst others enjoyed every moment and a long career. It was a tough job, out in all weathers, day and night, with little or no reward. Often, it also meant facing potential attack or abuse from an unforgiving public. Many men were simply unable to cope with the strict discipline and regimented, army-style routine. This particular incident however, seemed to have been blown out of all proportion and happened at a time when James was not in the best of health. The winter weather had taken its toll and, combined with the stress and strain of everyday duties and defending the action, he was forced to take some time off work to recover.

This is an honest account of what really happened to James, his co-defendants, and to the accuser. It is fully supported by press cuttings, court papers and the police archive records and reveals the 'behind the scenes' drama and incredible interest that the story provoked. It became a massive story too for the media with a so-called local hero facing ruin. The nationals also followed the story and it became one of the most important actions in police history at that time, dragging on for some time because of James's deteriorating health and therefore his inability to personally attend court in order to give evidence. I believe this final chapter in his story provides a most dramatic conclusion to the action-packed career of a dedicated and loyal servant; and this case perhaps acted as a sharp warning to both investigator and the accused. The actions also helped to create a new set of rules, regulations and guidelines that still remain in operation today. Based on the available evidence, this claim posed an unprecedented and totally unnecessary challenge by someone that James had previously helped in the past. It was also an unexpected attack from 'one of his own.' It became a shock from which James never recovered. Justice finally prevailed but at a very high price.

The case stemmed from   October 1913, when, some time after six o'clock in the evening, PC William Buckley was on patrol in Bury New Road, Strangeways, in the company of acting Sergeant Greenwood. He was approached by a local lad who said: 'What about that arrangement you have made with us tonight? Didn't you and PC 156 take our names and addresses last Thursday night and say – we will report you for obstruction, and then say, meet us on Saturday night in Bury New Road and give us a shilling each and we will let you off?' Buckley denied all knowledge of the 'arrangement' and the boy went away. The constable was later questioned about the incident by Superintendent Wood and then marched off to Derby Street police station, where he was placed in the reserve cell, searched and interrogated with regard to his police book. Wood's investigation was assisted by Sergeants Isaac Bennett and Thomas A. Court, both of Moston.

He [Buckley] accompanied the Superintendent to his (Buckley's) lodgings, where a search was made and a book was found, but not a police book. The matter was eventually investigated by the Chief Constable and in the sequel, Buckley was informed that no case had been made out against him. The case went before the Watch Committee, who did nothing in the matter.

Some months after Wood had completed his report into the incident, he and the two sergeants who had assisted him were sued by Buckley who claimed that the senior officers had assaulted him, unlawfully imprisoned him, caused his room to be broken into and entered and a book to be illegally removed.

FUNERAL OF SUPERINTEN-DENT WOOD.

Impressive Ceremony this Afternoon.

The funeral of Police Superintendent Wood took place, this afternoon, at Harpurhey Cemetery, and was witnessed by a large crowd, this being the first instance in the history of the Manchester police force that a superintendent on active service has died. The funeral procession left the deceased's residence in Newton Heath, headed by the police band playing the Dead March and a large body of police in charge of the acting superintendent of the division, Inspector Cubberley. Accompanying the cortege were the Chief Constable, Mr. R. Peacock, Chief Detective Superintendent Vaughan, and Superintendents Walker and Gilmour, both former superintendents of the B Division.

The cortege proceeded by way of Oldham Road, Lumb Lane, Queen's Road, to Harpurhey Cemetery. Six inspectors carried the body to the grave side: Inspectors Dentith, Grant, Harrison, and Lea (B Division), Liggett (E Division) and Webster (F Division).

The last rites were carried out by Inspector Webster. A large number of wreaths had been sent, including one from the Chief Constable, the Headquarters staff B Division, and other officers and men.

Newspaper report of James Wood's funeral.

Wood and the two sergeants denied the charges and defended their actions but the threat of legal action, the winter weather and the stress and strain of everyday duties forced Wood to take some time off work following the onset of some severe chest pains. The story was picked up by the press, not only locally, but nationally, and developed into a major story with a 'so-called local hero' facing ruin.

By March 1914, Wood was in Bournemouth trying to regain his health and the matter was adjourned for fear that a court appearance might have a detrimental effect upon him. The proceedings were delayed indefinitely and then, on 28 May, news was received that James Wood, who had returned from Bournemouth only two weeks earlier, had died at his home, the police station at 627 Oldham Road, Newton Heath, aged forty-six. The death certificate records that he died of an aortic aneurysm and heart failure.

His death was quickly followed by various tributes and acknowledgments in both local and national papers, the first appearing the following day, and began to reveal much more about his varied career. The funeral, held on 2 June 1914, became one of the largest ever in the city's history for any serving police officer within the Manchester Force, and practically closed all major roads in the area for several hours as colleagues and the general public paid their respects and joined a huge cortege, including the Manchester City Police Band, from his home at Newton Heath to Harpurhey Cemetery. The cortege proceeded by way of Oldham Road, Lumb Lane, and Queen's Road to Harpurhey Cemetery. Six inspectors (Dentith, Grant, Harrison and Lea of B Division; Liggett of E Division and Webster of F Division) carried the body to the graveside. The last rites were carried out by Inspector Webster. A large number of wreaths had been sent, including one from the Chief Constable, the headquarters staff and other officers and men.

In accordance with the practice of granting one month's pay for every completed year of approved service, his widow received a gratuity of £402 10s. (based on his salary of £210 per annum).

Despite the death of Wood, the legal case against him and the two sergeants was proceeded with in June 1914. Buckley claimed that Superintendent Wood examined Buckley's [note]book.

Nothing being found there, search was made for another book, which, it was suggested, was in the plaintiff's possession. Buckley, it was stated, was marched off to Derby Street police station between Wood and Bennett, and there he was placed in the reserve cell.

No police book was found either at Willert Street police station, or at Buckley's lodgings, where search was made, but another notebook, with some pages missing, was found, and afterwards Superintendent Wood told Buckley that he had been telling lies.

The other officer involved with Buckley in the matter was 'sufficiently badgered' … that he resigned and Buckley was also asked by the Superintendent if he had not better resign also, but he refused to do so.

Wood's evidence was presented to the court posthumously, via a transcript of an interview conducted by the judge.

Mr Wood told his Honour that he was the Superintendent of B Division and

Buckley was transferred to his division in the spring of 1913. Supt Wood referred to the complaints made by two Jewish lads last October that Buckley and the other Constable had agreed to accept a shilling on condition that they 'let off' the lads.

The Superintendent stated that the lads saw him and told him that the officers gave them to understand they might be summoned for obstruction unless they brought the money. The Supt went on to say that the youths were told to keep the appointment they alleged they had made with the Constables' and they were given a shilling (marked).

Later that evening, after Buckley had been seen speaking to the youths in the street, he was spoken to by Wood, who asked what the conversation had been about. Buckley told the Superintendent that he had not seen the youths before, and Wood then told him of the complaint the lads had made against him and asked him to go to the police station so that they might hear the boys make the complaint.

On the way to the station, Wood walked with Buckley, and Sergeant Bennett walked behind and Buckley was not in any sense in custody, as it was not the custom in the force to arrest officers without the consent of the Chief.

He was asked, when at the station to go into the reserve room so that the boys could not see him. When asked for his old police book, Buckley declared that he had given it up, but it was not found at Willert Street police station. Wood afterwards asked Sergeant Bennett to go through Buckley's pockets, but he took it that Buckley thoroughly consented to that step.

He (Wood) took a serious view of the allegation against Buckley, but he was anxious to clear him, if possible. Buckley himself assisted in the search, and if he had offered any objection, the search would not have continued. Buckley was allowed to question the lad who had made the charge against him.

The other officer involved in the matter with Buckley told Wood that he was determined to resign, and later Buckley also offered to resign, but after he had been told to think it over, he said he would stay on.

The defendants, Sergeants Bennett and Cort, in their evidence said that the plaintiff made no complaint or objection to what was done. The room called a reserve prisoner's cell was not a cell but a retiring room for the Sergeants' in the division. There was a gas jet in it, which made it unsuitable as a cell. ... They said that in all they did they acted under the instructions of their superior officer.

The judge decided that there had not been any wrongful arrest but regarding the search of the constable's home, the judge 'was not quite sure that it was the proper thing to do, but he was perfectly certain that the plaintiff sustained no damages as a consequence. He gave the judgement for the plaintiff for 20s., without costs'. The judge added: 'I can see no reason at all why he should have brought this action. The only doubt I had was whether to give judgement straight away for the defendants.'

Some small crumbs of comfort perhaps, but James was buried some sixteen days *before* the case was concluded. It had all seemed so totally unnecessary. And yet, the case caught the imagination of the press and public alike, who took James's personal tragedy to their hearts. It also became a cause, or case celebre within the force.

I know from personal records how bitterly disappointed James was, that his health problems prevented any court attendance, and that he was only allowed to provide evidence in a statement from a convalescent home in Bournemouth.

At least by this method, he felt he had finally exercised his duty. Both the Judge and the verdict exonerated James and his colleagues, but the action almost certainly helped accelerate his demise.

And who knows what would have happened to his health, had the case been concluded a month or two before this date? Certainly the stress, anxiety, and problems of preparing a defence in such a precarious state must have taken its toll.

Letitia Wood and her daughter were obliged to vacate the police house in Oldham Road. Bemused, bewildered, short of funds and future direction, she told the Watch Committee she would probably try to purchase a baby linen or drapery business in order to survive and help to support her daughter. And like James, she probably wondered what it had all been about.

James had been unfairly attacked by 'one of his own' and this was the particular point that hurt him and Letitia the most; and ironically it came from a man that James had tried to help before, after he had experienced some personal problems within the force. Not surprisingly, Buckley took the easy way out and hastily resigned from the force during the latter stages of the trial. He was certainly never heard of again and was thought to have left the area. It was claimed he made his decision as soon as he realised James had agreed to speak to the judge from his sick bed.

The sad part of this whole sordid affair, is that we will never know the real reasons why Buckley made these false claims, or quit the force at that particular time. Maybe he realised the game was up, and he was about to be 'found out,' then disciplined. Neither, we will ever know what would have happened to James and his family, had he lived a much longer life and continued to honour his employers in a similar fashion. It was a tragic end to a potentially glittering career but at least it is possible to record that he had made a very positive and invaluable contribution to the development of the police in Manchester.

Appendices

Appendix 1
Policing and living costs *c.*1900

Police wages: a police constable in 1900 would earn about £67 per year, which would increase to £80 after ten years service. A sergeant could expect to take home £104 per annum, and a superintendent about £290. Police officers could also apply for boot allowances of £1.50 per year and, if they ever reached the senior ranks, could also apply for rent allowances.

In comparison, general labourers earned £46 per annum, a railwayman about £43, and a shop assistant £20. In the higher bracket, a bank manager could expect about £400 per annum, and a music hall performer over £520 per annum. Rent and rates were high in comparison to wages and household accounts showed the regular purchase of lamp oil, washing soda, firewood, sticks, candles, black lead and scrubbing brushes. A loaf of bread was 3d, a pint of milk 1¹/2*d*., a pound of cheese 5*d*., sugar 1¹/4*d*. and a pound of potatoes ¹/2*d*. Coffee was expensive at 1*s*. and tea even worse at 1*s*. 5*d*. A newspaper varied in price from ¹/2*d*. to 1*d*., and seats at the theatre ranged from 6*d*. to 4*s*. Admission to the zoo cost 6*d*. A ride in a Hackney carriage (taxi) cost 9*d*. per mile and tram fares were about 3*d*. for a journey from the suburbs into the city centre. Horse tram fares were cheaper but were soon phased out with the introduction of trams powered by overhead electrcity. Many people used a variety of community-based clubs in order to purchase boots, clothing and essential supplies.

Appendix 2
Self Education for the Police, 1899

Another valuable document contained within James Wood's prized possessions was a small booklet entitled *Self Education for the Police*. It is about the size of a pocket notebook, with the title established in gold lettering on a black background. The first and last few inside pages are produced on a bright yellow coloured paper, with the following pages and main text printed on pale yellow and crème format material. There is a total of 142 pages which make for both fascinating and amusing reading, with interesting comparison to a long forgotten past.

The book (compiled by a H. Childs, who is shown in the book as a trained certified schoolmaster) was first published at the office of the *Police Review & Parade Gossip*, at 18 Catherine Street, Strand, London, in 1899. It is basically a police rulebook of the day, with twenty-four suggested skeleton reports and further tests and suggestions for dealing with a whole range of expected scenarios to help prepare and guide any 'rookie and totally bewildered policeman'. The index for the reports reflects and discusses a variety of matters pertinent to that developing era including:

A collision between an omnibus and hansom cab, the removal of a lunatic, an obstruction of public gathering outside a hall, a fatal accident on ice, a horse taken ill, an accident to the driver of an omnibus, accident relating to a defective coal shoot, a man knocked down by a cyclist, man bitten by a dog, false alarm of fire, the searching of a servant's box and various forms of suicides and other imponderable misadventures.

In addition, it includes sections on special self-examination questions about the law; spelling tests; difficult words that are pronounced alike, or nearly alike, but are different in meaning; catchy words taken from previous examination papers for the purposes of revision; challenging dictation tests; and arithmetic.

The novice policeman at the turn of the twentieth century was obviously expected to be a highly proficient and knowledgeable citizen, much respected within his local community. It was demanded by his employers that he should be able to take charge of a number of potentially volatile and everyday situations, and be able to act on his own initiative, as assistance in those days was often delayed and initially only summoned by use of a wooden rattle, then later, a police whistle.

The depth of information within *Self Education for the Police* confirmed all the expectations and demanding duties of a police officer. The special examination questions were challenging to say the least, but once learnt were probably never forgotten and this book fast became an essential aid and a 'Bobbies Bible' for all occasions, confirming both the law of the land and a policeman's responsibilities, with, and to the general public.

The book also included guidance on what a police officer should do about various situations including burglary, common assault, the serving of beer & spirits, alarm of fire, a wandering lunatic, murder, prostitution, house-breaking, fireworks, locomotives, vehicles on the highway, annoyance by a horse dealer, the arrest of a Peer or MP, and a host of other important and essential matters.

It contained a couple of dozen reports of lessons, and the same amount of special examination questions. The arithmetic tests were demanding and included detailed sections on numeration, notation, subtraction, division, multiplication, weights and measures, compound fractions and many more. The most notable weights & measures used in 1899 were ounces, pounds, quarters, stones, hundredweights and tons; long measures were feet, inches, yards, poles furlongs, chains, fathoms, nautical miles or knots and weights included grains, pennyweights, ounces, pounds, stones, hundredweights and tons. There was also guidance on cloth measure (inches, nails, quarters, yards), apothecaries weights (grains, scruples, drams, ounces and pounds), square measures (square inches, feet, feet, yards, poles, perches, roods, rods, acres and square miles), dry measures (gills, pints, quarts, gallons, pecks, bushels, quarters and loads), coal & coke measures (pecks, bushels, sacks and chaldrons), time, paper measures (sheets, quires, reams, bales) and liquid measures (gills, pints, quarts, gallons, firkin, kilderkin, barrel, hogshead, butt and an anker of wine). Knowledge of these tables helped officers to quickly deal with any potential disputes for trading, deliveries or supply, and generally related to coal and coke, or those of an alcoholic nature.

Spelling, English and vocabulary, similarly a knowledge of mathematical tables was considered of vital importance; hence the preparation of editorial matters by a qualified schoolmaster.

Below are some interesting key examples taken from the special skeleton police incident reports at the turn of the century from a fascinating generous index, they include, amongst others:

Lesson I

Collision between an omnibus and a hansom cab. The horse in the hansom cab is injured and afterwards has to be killed ... the report suggest how the police officer should record the incident. It begins:

I beg to report that at ... (pm) ... inst, a collision occurred at the junction of ... (street or road) and ... (road or thoroughfare), between omnibus ... (plate no.) ... (driver's badge no.) .... (conductor's badge no.) .... (hansom cab no.) ... (plate no.) ... (driver's badge no.).

The collision was caused by the driver of latter vehicle turning too sharply from ... (street) ... into ... (street) and colliding with former vehicle before the driver could pull out of the way, The horse attached to hansom cab was thrown down, breaking both fore-legs.

I immediately sent for Mr ... (name). The veterinary surgeon of ... (address), who on arrival, caused the animal to be slaughtered and removed. I sent information of the occurrence to ... (name), of ... (address), the owner of the horse and hansom cab, and at ... (pm), men in his employ attended and removed the cab.

In the meantime, with the assistance of PC ... (number) ... I diverted traffic by way of ... (street or road), and ... (street or road). At ... (pm), the traffic resumed its normal course. No other damage or casualties. Witnessed, and no expenses incurred by PC ... Reporting. Name ... Date ... .

Lesson VI

A PC has been called to a private house where a person has been assaulted.

State fully what steps should be taken (This is also marked as an examination question). The skeleton report begins:

PC ... (No.) ... (name), reports that at ... (am) ... inst ... he was called by ... (name) ... (address) ... to a private house . ... (address) ... by ... (name). ... a lodger in the same house had assaulted him with an umbrella.
There being no marks of violence PC ... referred the complaint to a Magistrate for a summons.

Some other examples with pre-written reports are:

Lesson VIII
PC called to a private house to assist in the removal of a lunatic to the Infirmary. (Marked as an examination question).

PC ... (No.) ... (name) ... , reports that at ... (pm) ... Inst, while passing (number) ... (address), parish of ... (name), the relieving officer for the District called him and asked for his assistance in the removal of ... (name), a lunatic, from above address to ... (Infirmary) ... (street or road), as he could not manage him himself.
PC being shown the order for the order for above removal immediately assisted, and the lunatic was conveyed in four-wheeled cab, plate no .... (driver's badge no) ... to the above Infirmary, where he was placed under restraint.

Lesson XIV
Horse suddenly taken ill in the street.
PC ... (No.) ... (name) ... , reports that at ... (time) ... (date) ... While on duty in ... (street or road), his attention was called to a horse attached to a cart, owned and driven by ... (name and address). The horse, which was in good condition and bore no marks of ill usage, had been taken suddenly ill while passing along the above street, and appeared to be in great pain.
PC sent for ... (Veterinary Surgeon) ... (address) ... who stated that animal was suffering from cramp in the stomach. No blame was attached to the driver. In a short time, the animal was sufficiently recovered to be taken home by owner (as above). Witnessed by PC ... (No.) ... Expenses incurred, owner paying veterinary surgeon.

Lesson XV
PC injured on duty.

I beg to report that at … pm … Inst, while on duty in … (street or road), parish of … I heard shouts of 'stop him' and saw a horse attached to a light spring cart, with a bicycle entangled in the near side wheel, being driven at a furious rate along the above road.

I immediately called upon the driver to stop, and ran into the roadway and held up my hands with a view to stopping the horse; but the driver whipped the horse and urged it on. I then endeavoured to catch hold of the reigns and, in doing so, was knocked down, the near wheel of the cart passing over my left leg, thereby injuring the same.

The horse was stopped by PC … (No.) … (name) … when it was found that the driver … (name) … (age) … of (address) … was drunk, and that he had previously collided with a bicycle belonging to … (name) … (address) … Which had been left standing by the kerb in above thoroughfare, the owner of which machine had immediately pursued the cart, and cried out 'stop him!'

The driver was then taken into custody by PC … (as above), and charged with being drunk and furiously driving to the common danger of the public, thereby causing actual bodily harm to myself. I was subsequently seen by the Divisional Surgeon, who certified me to be suffering from severe bruises to left leg, and directed me to be placed on the sick list.

Lesson XIX
A fatal accident occurs through a defective coal-shoot, and while proceeding to the spot, cries of 'murder' are heard proceeding from the third floor of a house in the same street. What steps would you take?

PC … (No.) … (name) … reports that at … (pm) … inst, while on duty in … (street or road), parish of … (name), he was informed by … (name … of (place), that a man had fallen over a coal-shoot in front of … (address), and while proceeding there, he heard cries of 'murder' coming from the third floor of No. … (same street).

PC … (No.) … (name) … Coming up at the time, was directed by PC reporting to see the injured man while he entered the house where the cries proceeded from, and on entering a room on third floor found ….

(name), the former being drunk. On being questioned by PC, the wife stated that her husband, being drunk and quarrelsome, having threatened to strike her, she had screamed 'murder' to frighten him.

Seeing that no breach of the peace was likely to happen, PC left the premises and proceeded to … (hospital), and on enquiring of the house surgeon respecting the injured man, as above, was told that he had several ribs broken, and had died shortly after admission from severe shock to the system.

Body now in hospital mortuary to await inquest. On the body was found a card bearing the following name and address … (name) … (address). Friends and Coroner's office informed. Body subsequently identified by his wife. Owner of coal-shoot seen, who stated that coals had been delivered at his house that day, and that the plate must have been insecurely fastened, but was thoroughly secure now.

Lesson XXI
A man carrying a plank on his shoulder, while crossing a street is knocked down by a bicyclist. State steps taken.

PC … (No.) … (name) … reports that at … (time) … (date) … finding … (name) … (age) … of … (address) … labourer in the employ of Messrs … (name & address), builders, lying on the pavement in …. (street or road), parish of … (name), bleeding from a wound on the right hand side of his head and suffering from an injury to his right shoulder.

PC at once sent to station for ambulance and conveyed him to … (hospital), where he was seen by Dr … (name), house surgeon, who stated that he was suffering from a severe scalp wound and dislocated right shoulder, and detained him in bed … (No.) … (ward) … (name).

The injured man stated that as he was crossing the above street with a plank on his shoulder, he was knocked down by a bicycle, rider unknown, who rode away at a furious pace in the direction of … (place), and he was unable to give any description of him. PC made enquiries in the neighbourhood but was unable to find anyone who witnessed the occurrence. Friends and employer informed, and no expenses incurred by PC reporting.

Lesson XXIII
PC called by a lady, who wished him to search the box of a servant, whom she suspects has stolen some linen.

PC … (No.) … (name) … reports that at … (time) … (date), while on duty in … (street or road) … (parish or district), he was called by Mrs … (name) of same street, who requested him to search a box, which was standing in the hall, belonging to … (name), who was just leaving her employ, and whom she suspected had stolen some table cloths, pillow cases and table napkins and had hidden them in the box (as above). PC informed complainant that he had no authority to comply with her request, and referred her to a Magistrate; but advised her to ascertain, if possible, where the box was to be conveyed, in case of future proceedings.

Some of the special examination questions too were designed to test the policeman's knowledge of everyday situations. I have enjoyed reviewing a selection of the tests in the book and have selected twenty questions relevant to that period. They include: -

1) What must the damage to shrubs in a garden amount to before you could arrest?
2) What age must a person be before a publican can serve him with sprits, to be consumed on the premises? Also beer?
3) If you found a person insensible in the street, what steps would you take?
4) If you found the door of a dwelling house open at night, what would you do?
5) If several persons complained to you of great annoyance caused by a man employed at a horse dealer's close by. What would you do?
6) What do you mean by 'night?'
7) If the conductor of a tramcar called you to a man who refused to pay his fare, which he said he had already done, but could produce no ticket, what steps would you take?
8) During which time is a bicyclist bound to have his lamp alight?
9) If a person is committing a nuisance in a public thoroughfare, what is necessary before you can arrest?
10) During what time is a locomotive prohibited from passing through the streets of the Metropolis?

11) After what length of time, dating from time of injuries received, cannot a person be charged with 'murder?'

12) How many vehicles may one person, at one time, drive along a highway, before chargeable, and under what conditions?

13) What is a 'Common Lodging House?'

14) If you saw a woman whom you know to be a prostitute accost a gentleman in the street and could not hear what she said, but saw him waive her away with his hand, what steps would you take? And if you saw her repeat it, what would you do?

15) If a lodger in a house commits suicide, and the occupier wishes you to remove the dead body to the mortuary, would you do so?

16) What steps would you take if the landlord of a public house wanted to give a person into custody for refusing to quit?

17) At what time must an unlicensed refreshment house close?

18) If a person wished to bring an action against the police what must he or she do first? And after what lapse of time would it not be valid?

19) If you were on duty and saw an omnibus driver stop on a crossing would you order the driver to pull up higher, or what would you do?

20) If a person offered you the keys of his premises, which are on your beat, and requested you to go in occasionally to see that all was safe, what would you do?

In the latter part of the book and due to the economic and political climate of the time, the policeman was fast required to have specific knowledge of many key issues that could occur during the course of everyday duties. Some of these included:

1) For what offences can a Peer or MP and their servants be arrested? A: For treason, felony and breach of the peace.

2) When can an Ambassador or suite be arrested? A: For an attempt on the life of the Sovereign.

3) Can a private person arrest? If so, when and when not? A: When a felony is being committed, and he sees it taking place, or sees a dangerous wound given. If under 21-years of age, he cannot be arrested. [A felony was described as a more serious offence than misdemeanour and includes murder and attempts to murder and maim, rape, manslaughter, robbery and attempted robbery, burglary

and housebreaking, cattle, horse and sheep stealing, receiving stolen goods, embezzlement, arson, nearly all cases of forging and coining, and assaults when armed.]